Tell the Truth

The Whole Gospel to the Whole Person by Whole People

*A Training Manual on
the Message and Methods
of God-centered Witnessing*

Will Metzger

*InterVarsity Press
Downers Grove
Illinois 60515*

InterVarsity Press is the book-publishing division of Inter-Varsity Christian Fellowship, a student movement active on campus at hundreds of universities, colleges and schools of nursing. For information about local and regional activities, write IVCF, 233 Langdon St., Madison, WI 53703.

"Meet My Friend" reprinted by permission from a tract, Good News Publishers, Westchester, Illinois 60153.

"What Is Your Favorite Game?" by Dr. George Sweeting, Moody Press, Moody Bible Institute of Chicago. Used by permission.

"You're a Beautiful Person" by David Smith, Moody Press, Moody Bible Institute of Chicago. Used by permission.

ISBN 0-87784-934-X

Printed in the United States of America

Library of Congress Cataloging in Publication Data

Metzger, Will, 1940-
   Tell the truth.

   Includes bibliographical references.
   1. Witness bearing (Christianity) 2. Evangelistic work. I. Title.
BV4520.M47   1984   248'.5   83-25304
ISBN 0-87784-934-X

17   16   15   14   13   12   11   10   9
98   97   96   95

Acknowledgments

*What follows is motivated by
a desire to help others and
a sense of debt owed to:*
God
*for his glorious, gracious and
free salvation;*
My Teachers
*for the rich heritage of
Christian truth they have
passed on to me
through their words and
writings;*
My Family and Friends
*for helping me see that truth
is not theoretical.*

Introduction

The Whole Gospel to the Whole Person by Whole People: Our Task in Evangelism

You know how I lived the whole time I was with you, from the first day I came into the province of Asia. I served the Lord with great humility and with tears, although I was severely tested by the plots of the Jews. You know that I have not hesitated to preach anything that would be helpful to you but have taught you publicly and from house to house. I have declared to both Jews and Greeks that they must turn to God in repentance and have faith in our Lord Jesus . . . I consider my life worth nothing to me, if only I may finish the race and complete the task the Lord Jesus has given me—the task of testifying to the gospel of God's grace. . . . For I have not hesitated to proclaim to you the whole will of God.
Acts 20:18-22, 24, 27

Have you ever been stymied by evangelism? Do you feel you are tossed between two unacceptable alternatives and can't find your niche? On the one side you see Christians who are very friendly to others, but don't say much about Jesus Christ. On the other side are those who are always "giving out the gospel" but seem to know nothing about genuine friendship. The frustration of bumping into these two extremes in Christian circles is very real.

This book is designed to help you tell the gospel in a way honoring to God, helpful to others and liberating for you. It is neither a plan for buttonholing people nor a plea for being "just a good guy" who lets others come to you if and when they want to talk religion. Rather, its goal is to help you recover the theological content of the gospel because only as your view of God is changed can you find the confidence, joy and gratitude to undergird a new evangelistic lifestyle.

At First It Seemed So Simple

I was one of those Christians who believed in friendship evangelism, but for me it turned out to be all friendship and little evangelism. Motivation was not a problem for me. I had gone through a life-changing conversion to Christ during my high-school years, and Jesus Christ was very real to me. I had a strong desire to tell others about him, yet most of my models for doing so tended toward one or the other of the extremes I mentioned above. I had other liabilities in addition to those examples: my own lack of Bible knowledge, my personal immaturity and my tendency to view God as existing only for my benefit. With those drawbacks I began my personal pilgrimage to find out what it meant to be a witness for Christ.

At first, witnessing seemed so simple. I knew the message and I knew who needed it. What could be so confusing or difficult about that? All too soon, I found out.

I was soon beset by a barrage of advice. First I was told I should witness by showing others a good time: I should bring my high-school acquaintances to fun gatherings in the inoffensive setting of a home. The evening would end with a challenging talk. That sounded legitimate.

But then in college I met Christians who emphasized a more direct approach: I should invite anyone and everyone to a small group Bible study (sometimes a talk by a layperson in a "neutral" setting). Nonbelievers should be confronted openly with the Scriptures. "Well," I said to myself, "that sounds reasonable. Perhaps *this* is the approach to take."

Not too much later my confusion was intensified because I came in contact with still other Christians who exhorted me to evangelize by the apostolic pattern of preaching: I should bring my friends to hear gifted speakers at church, special meetings or on TV.

And then I had a grand awakening. I saw that *I* was to witness—not just bring people to others who would witness for me. Fearful, and yet convinced of my duty, I looked for help. Again, I met some Christians who were very zealous and explained to me an entirely *new* set of ideas and techniques for personal evangelism. I was motivated by an awesome sense of responsibility and increasing guilt because I was led to believe that I was unspiritual—or at least unfaithful—if I hadn't "led someone to Christ." So I uncritically grabbed onto various methods of witnessing. I began to feel obligated to speak to every person who crossed my path. Unless I resorted to this prepackaged form of "giving them the gospel," I felt like a failure. While this approach did involve me in speaking the truth to others, it seemed so impersonal and mechanical. Something was still missing.

I began to question the salesmanship approach. I wasn't sure it fit the concept of God I found in the Scriptures. Because many of my friends agreed with me, they decided not to witness at all. But I knew this was not the answer either. I had started out with misgivings about the appropriateness of the slick techniques advocated by various "successful" evangelists. I ended up with misgivings as to whether they fit in with Scripture. My questions led me to some basic questions of theology.

Doubts whirled in my mind. Could a person be motivated to witness, yet actually dishonor God and misrepresent his message through ignorance or manipulation? Was I motivated by guilt, or the expectations of others? Was I trying to make excuses for my lack of enthusiasm and success? How could I limit God's use of me to just "friends" and "invitations to meetings"? How could I deny that since most of the people I met were going to perish, I should speak to everyone I could?

I began to feel like I was caught in a revolving door. Certain questions kept twirling me around. In what way am I obligated to those (even strangers) God brings across my path? Why are the converts of different Christian groups often distinguished by certain personality types? Am I evangelizing only when I see conversions? What are the essential elements of our message? Do I unite with others in evangelism because of the need of people to hear or because of a mutual commitment to certain doctrines? Why is there such reticence to examine the biblical basis for methods of witness (especially if they are the ones our group uses)?

Why is there such disagreement, confusion, and vagueness among those who witness, even on some very basic elements of the gospel, such as: Do we just present Christ as Savior or also as Lord to the unbeliever? Is repentance and teaching the law of God part of the gospel? Why is the new birth necessary? What actually happens in the new birth? What is our part in salvation and what is God's? How can a person know he or she has been born again? The gospel—is it a set of doctrines or a person?

It boggled my mind that, once Christians passed beyond the common notion that everyone needs Christ for salvation, there was confusion and even contradiction on what the new birth really meant. These are haunting, important, fundamental questions. How could the majority of evangelicals be so oblivious to the need to recover the biblical gospel? I could see there were many wrong methods, and I began to despair that I could ever find a way to witness that would take its shape from the truth.

All my questions could be boiled down to one: what was the right way to witness?

My first five years as a Christian were beset with concern about witnessing. I know many can identify with me. Now the ultimate question remains—can we find any definitive solution?

In spite of the unhelpfulness of the advice initially given to me about personal evangelism, I have to admit that the resurgent interest in this topic in evangelical circles is healthy. Who can deny that there has been an increased participation in evangelism? Who could find fault with the new evangelistic concern of many Christians? They have made great sacrifices in money, time and energy. People are using modern media creatively. I am truly thankful for these things. Yet, something bothers me—and I believe others also have an uneasy conscience. Could some aspects of contemporary evangelism lack biblical integrity?

The Virtue of Evaluation
Before we can find an answer to this central question we must

evaluate the current practices in evangelism. Let me paraphrase Dr. Francis Schaeffer's address before the World Congress on Evangelism in Berlin: It is just because we are committed to evangelism that we must speak in antithesis at times. If we do not make clear by word and practice our position for truth and against false doctrine, we are building a wall between the next generation and the gospel. The unity of evangelicals should be on the basis of truth and not on evangelism as such. If this is not so, "success" in evangelism can result in weakening Christianity. Any consideration of methods is secondary to this central principle.

Though we need to evaluate doctrine and methods, however, we are not to judge the motives of others; so in part one of this book I will pose pertinent questions concerning the *theology* underlying the methodology in modern evangelism. I do not pretend to give an exhaustive theology of evangelism. I speak as a family member to those within the family of God. May we all look into our hearts and into the Bible to find how to be better witnesses. I hope that my analysis will lead to constructive dialog and change for all of us. Should any tradition, technique or person be beyond our evaluation by scriptural standards? I think not.

If it is true that there are serious differences among evangelicals on the message and methods of evangelism, then we must ask to what extent are these differences justified? If the differences are simply due to the different audience we are reaching or the variety of gifts God has given us, these differences are not bad. But if in evangelism we are just being loyal to our tradition, molding truth to our personality, diluting the gospel or manipulating people, we are wrong. Let us be willing to reexamine our theology of evangelism by Scripture, for otherwise our evangelism may be infected by prejudice, pragmatism and sin. If, however, we are convinced there is a *theological* reason behind our methodology, then we *may* be justified in evangelizing accordingly. Then our difference is a matter of our conscience bound by what we conceive Scripture teaches. A scriptural doctrine of evangelism should be the controlling element in any practice of evangelism.

Nevertheless, even when we can articulate a theological base for our evangelism, I do not believe our responsibility has ended until we compare our doctrinal interpretation with that of others and in humility be willing to rethink what the Holy Spirit is telling us in Scripture. Not to do so is to say that we cannot learn from each other. It is to deny that new light can break forth upon our understanding of the Scripture. It is to limit the Holy Spirit in communicating to us from other Christians. It is to evangelize a certain way out of tradition and not out of conviction.

In short, to be unwilling to evaluate our evangelism in the light of the Bible is not to take Scripture seriously. We could end up being less than honest with each other, allowing unbelievers to be misled and frustrating those who wish to learn to witness. We could condemn our children and the church to untold problems. We could be dishonoring the God of the gospel. We must take a thorough look at current evangelistic practice to see if those who witness to Christ have a balanced and whole gospel.

In part two, then, I consider what the total effect of the gospel should be on our lives and on the lives of those we evangelize. Evaluation is again necessary and right in order to determine why there are so many "partial" conversions. A commitment to Christ is not a mere prayer and that's it. Rather it is a conversion in the true sense of the word. Our whole lives are changed. Paul says we become new creations. I discuss how this change must affect our entire being; our minds, our wills and our emotions.

But our responsibility does not end with correct understanding of the new birth. We must put that gospel into action. We are called to obedience in telling the truth to others. Therefore, part three is devoted to the practice of witnessing, plus some ideas on how to get started. Worksheets are included to help you improve your witness and lead an evangelism training seminar for others.

Evangelism: Person to Person

I have intentionally confined my subject to personal witnessing. This is not because other forms are invalid but because, as the evangelical statesman Dr. Carl Henry contends, a one-to-one approach initiated by every believer still holds the best promise of evangelizing the earth in our century.[1] Yale historian Kenneth S. Latourette reinforces this concept when he reminds us that "The chief agents in the expansion of Christianity appear not to have been those who made it a profession . . . , but men and women who carried on their livelihood in some purely secular manner and spoke of their faith to those they met in this natural fashion."[2]

Some may question the validity of stressing person-to-person evangelism. Perhaps their questions stem from abuses of this approach. The "Lone Ranger" mentality can also foster it. An unbiblical individualism has made some people promote exclusively the corporate nature of Christian witness. "May they be brought to complete unity *to let the world know* that you sent me and have loved them even as you have loved me" (Jn. 17:23). The body of believers united out of various economic and ethnic backgrounds while retaining individual personalities and interests should be like a flashing neon sign to the world. The amazing unity in the diversity of Christ's body can convince unbelievers that Jesus Christ was sent by God. A dynamic group of vibrant Christians forms the base for ongoing evangelism, *yet* if individuals in the group are not verbalizing the gospel, the net result will still be weak evangelism (see appendix A under "Corporate Witness").

In Scripture we find many examples of the gospel being spread in a person-to-person fashion. Jesus himself constantly converses with people to whom he is providentially led. He brings the word of life to them in the midst of their daily life. Christ promises the disciples that they will become fishers of men and then sends them out twice in pairs to spread the glad tidings (Mk. 6:7-13; Lk. 10:1-24). In the early church the average Christian is involved in evangelism (Acts 8:1, 4). A leader in the church, Philip, is commanded by God to leave a successful ministry in order to speak to an individual who is searching (Acts 8:26-40). Paul emphasizes the responsibility of all believers to be Christ's ambassadors and says that the ministry of reconciliation has been given to them

(2 Cor. 5:17-20). God gives greater ability in evangelism to certain people not in order that they might do it all but in order to equip each believer in the body to do this ministry (Eph. 4:11-12).

In the workaday world there are relatively few instances in which a person is converted apart from the help of an individual conversing with him. God's new birth usually involves us as spiritual midwives. Like little children we "show and tell" the gospel. Inherent in every approach to evangelism (small group Bible study, preaching, use of various media and so on) is the need for personal encounter. More often than not, an individual must speak with the non-Christian in order to clarify and urge him to believe. Aren't you a believer today because someone reached out personally to you? This is not to deny the validity and usefulness of other methods (especially preaching), which I mention in appendix A. However, it is *we* who are constituted Christ's ambassadors, and it is *we* whom God appoints to tell the gospel.

In conclusion, let me add a word of encouragement to those struggling with being faithful in evangelism. Nothing has the potential for producing more guilt among Christians than this subject (unless it's sex!). I can guarantee the reaction I will get when I speak on this topic: eyes lower, feet shuffle, hands fidget. There is usually some tension-releasing laughter. But all these reactions are unnecessary. There is hope, encouragement and liberation to be found when evangelism is built on a God-centered gospel. The doorway into a hopeful and joyful witness is found by focusing on God as Creator and Redeemer.

At the outset of this study I will lay a theological foundation under the heading of "The Whole Gospel." The platform on which we can build a life of evangelism will be God's sovereignty. We shall see the skillful interweaving of each person of the Trinity working in harmony in salvation. God has chosen. Christ has accomplished. The Spirit will inevitably apply. God always goes before us as we witness. As we learn and tell the truth, we experience theology turning into doxology.

Part I

The Whole Gospel: Content of Our Message

Paul then stood up in the meeting of the Areopagus and said: "Men of Athens! I see that in every way you are very religious. For as I walked around and observed your objects of worship, I found even an altar with this inscription: TO AN UNKNOWN GOD. Now what you worship as something unknown I am going to proclaim to you.

"The God who made the world and everything in it is the Lord of heaven and earth and does not live in temples built by hands. And he is not served by human hands, as if he needed anything, because he himself gives all men life and breath and everything else. From one man he made every nation of men, that they should inhabit the whole earth; and he determined the times set for them and the exact places where they should live. God did this so that men would seek him and perhaps reach out for him and find him, though he is not far from each one of us. 'For in him we live and move and have our being.' As some of your own poets have said, 'We are his children.'

"Therefore since we are God's children, we should not think that the divine being is like gold or silver or stone—an image made by man's design and skill. In the past God overlooked such ignorance but now he commands all people everywhere to repent. For he has set a day when he will judge the world with justice by the man he has appointed. He has given proof of this to all men by raising him from the dead."
Acts 17:22-31

1

Personal Witness as Sowing and Watering

I waited expectantly as the speaker began his comments. His topic was evangelism. I was taken aback when he started using the phrase "soul winning" to describe his evangelistic practice. "Okay," I thought to myself, "so this impersonal phrase grates you. Let's see if the rest of the talk gets any better." It didn't. What followed was a string of success stories about people he had led to Christ. He reinforced his point by citing famous stars and athletes as victorious evangelists. Then came an emphasis on techniques and manipulation of people reminiscent of cults I had studied.

His crowning illustration of how to "get the gospel out to every person" was a detailed set of instructions on how to roll up a gospel tract in such a way that it could be accurately dropped from the window of a moving car. The object was for it to drift to the feet of a hitchhiker—as you passed him by! He justified this technique on the basis of the startling story of a young man who was converted by this sort of "gospel bomb." The speaker's conclusion, "It works," sounded to me like the unbiblical idea, "the end justifies the means." As I left the church that night I wondered, "Instead of sending his Son, why didn't God just send a tract?"

What Is Witness?

We have good cause to wonder what kind of a gospel is being conveyed in our day. I am referring not only to individual speakers (this man was a professor of evangelism at a Christian school), but to seminars and books that purport to train Christians in evangelism. I'm embarrassed at the shoddy methods and anemic view of God prevalent among many of my Christian friends. We need a growing concern for a God-honoring witness to his own gospel. Before we can make any headway, however, we should define our terms. What do we mean by *evangelism* and *witness?*

In thinking of witnessing, we have to walk between a narrow and a broad definition. Narrowly defined, witnessing is confined to a rehearsal of a few gospel facts in the hearing of a nonbeliever. Broadly defined, it is whatever we do as Christians before the world. Neither of these definitions is satisfactory. The first narrows witness to only our lips; the second broadens it to our life. But it is our words *and* our ways that are inextricably bound together in witness. It is easy to excuse ourselves by saying either, "Well, I told him the gospel!" or, "I just live my life before others." It seems these two extremes have developed more in reaction to each other than on any biblical basis. What might be a more balanced view?

The chief end of each man and woman is not "to be a super soul-winner night and day." As the Westminster Catechism says, it is "to glorify God and enjoy Him forever." This means that we, as whole people, are to know God and keep God in focus in all that we do. Clearly, the way we live is a primary aspect of our witness. Yet our life is to be coupled with telling God's truth. People need to be told who it is who makes our lives different. Our lives, then, will illuminate the truth we express to nonbelievers. The airplane of Christian witness always has two wings: our lives (conduct) and our lips (conversation).

To remain silent and let others put their interpretation upon our actions is wrong. God himself did not do this. The great pivotal points of God's redemptive action in history are accompanied with verbal revelation. God wants us to understand the meaning of his actions. Likewise we must speak—and speak of Christ—even if we sense our own inconsistency of life. We must speak even when we do not know much about the Bible. We must speak even when it is inconvenient. God is bigger than our sins, our ignorance, our pride. He will honor his word in our mouths.

Nevertheless, at times our actions do speak louder than our words. When John describes our commission to witness, he says that as the Father sent the Son, in the same manner we are sent to others (Jn. 20:21). God didn't send a tract, he prepared a body. Likewise, God has prepared our bodies to demonstrate him. We need to be creative and selfless in our love to others. We need to learn how to be friends as well as perceive the needs of others and *do* something for them. Much of Jesus' witness was in response to a question *following* an act of kindness or a miracle. But we need to make sure that we are not condescending. We should allow others to help us, let them minister to us. Jesus asked the Samaritan woman to give him some water. We need to learn to be human and treat others as God's image bearers. If we are friendly only as long as the unbeliever is interested in discussing the gospel, we don't know much about friendship. We need to listen and seek to serve, not just talk.

How does the Bible define witnessing? In the Great Commission as expressed by Luke, we have central truths to which we are witnesses (Lk. 24:48). At the ascension, Christ's last words command the disciples to witness about him, a person (Acts 1:8). In the Gospels we see the writers selecting incidents from the life of Christ to convey the gospel. The background for the word *witness* is the law court. To witness is to testify that Christ is who he said he is. Such testimony is a means to an end—to give an eyewitness account of the truth (1 Jn. 1:1-3).

The Difference between Witness and Testimony

The content is Christ and God, not our journey to faith. Our personal testimony may be included, but witnessing is more than reciting our spiritual autobiography. Specific truths about a specific person are the subject of our proclamation. A message has been committed to us—a *word* of reconciliation to the world (2 Cor. 5:19).

Good evaluation questions to keep in mind after hearing a testimony are, "How much did I learn about Christ? How much about the speaker? Which was more prominent?" When people are very much in love, you find them expressing many things about their loved one and not always focusing on themselves. I still remember the change that came over an especially shy girl every time she got the chance to talk about her boyfriend. You couldn't keep her quiet! It is the same with a healthy testimony about our lover—Christ. (See appendix B, worksheet 2.)

Why is it important to distinguish between *witness* and *testimony?* In an age of religious pluralism, we find many who are testifying. I'll never forget the time when I had been speaking to a young man about the change Christ had made in my life. His sincere response was, "Transcendental Meditation does the same for me." What would you have said in reply? Some people recommend faith in a guru or in a technique of meditation or in self or in relationships. Many cite experiences of a change in life. If our witness has no more content than this, we can expect the typical response: "That's interesting. I'm glad for you, but what you have isn't for me."

Faith is not to be looked on as a separate entity ("I wish I had your faith"), but as an instrument given by God that is valid only because it has an object worthy of that faith—Jesus Christ. "It is worth noting that the New Testament Christians never attempted to establish the truth of Christianity on their inward experiences. . . . To put it another way, never do we find Paul trying to prove the truth of Christianity to others 'because of the difference it has made in my life.' "[1]

Do Results Count?

The crucial thing to remember in evangelism is the distinction between our responsibility and God's. Our task is to present faithfully the gospel message by our lives and our lips.[2] Any definition of our task that includes results is confusing our responsibility with God's prerogative, which is regeneration. Picture a fragile, thin-stemmed wine glass. Now think of a rock the size of a basketball. Imagine lifting that rock and dropping it into that delicately constructed glass. Shattered. We too will be broken if we try to carry something that only God can carry. We sow and water; God gives the increase (1 Cor. 3:5-9). We *may* reap—but only when God has brought the grain to maturity.

The question of whether or not we are evangelizing cannot be settled by counting the number of converts. In that case, many faithful missionaries who have seen no converts from years of labor would have to be rebuked for lack of witnessing. To define evangelism in terms of results is too broad. Then its essence becomes a quantitative procedure. If no results, then no evangelism has been done. I do not mean to suggest we should not evaluate both our results and nonresults, building a holy dissatisfaction with nonresults. We are not content with fishing yet never catching any fish (Lk. 5:4-11) or having empty seats at God's kingdom banquet (Lk. 14:15-24).

It is just as misleading to narrow our definition of evangelism to the type of meeting, literature, appeal or Bible passage used. If we did this, then we would be embarrassed to find no evangelism done in the New Testament times. Can you imagine trying to find a biblical example of today's typical evangelistic rally and appeal?[3] Rather, we need to evaluate all supposed evangelism by the question "What truth was taught?" If we think wrongly about our definition of evangelism, we are likely to act wrongly in our methods of evangelism.

In the Bible we have many examples of witnessing and many principles we can draw from them. We can study the way Jesus interacted with people and the way the apostles witnessed in the

Spirit. By studying these models, we can be helped in our own witness. From these, however, I will mention only one as I conclude a definition of witnessing. The passage is an account of Paul's witness before Agrippa (Acts 26:16-29). It highlights the characteristic of bold, conscience-directed speech.

In this passage Paul describes himself as appointed by God as a servant and a witness (a good combination to keep in mind). In a series of striking contrasts, the goal of his mission is summarized as nothing less than conversion. Repentance and evidence of it were his major concerns. Paul centers on fulfillment of Scripture and Christ's death and resurrection. He speaks to Agrippa's conscience—an element often neglected in witnessing. This same directness in which Paul uses the accusation "you know" is found in Acts 20:17-27—this time before Christians. Genuine witnessing involves persuading people to convert, but stops short of evaluating the success only in terms of results.

There are two main ways that we can study the presentation of the gospel. First, we can study the Bible itself, especially the book of Acts, the Epistles, and the life of Christ. Second, we can study the history of the Christian church. That is, we look at the revivals and in particular the people whose preaching has been honored in the conversion of others.

From such study, Dr. Lloyd-Jones has drawn the following foundational principles for evangelism:

1. The supreme object of the work of evangelism is to glorify God, not to save souls.

2. The only power that can do this work is the Holy Spirit, not our own strength.

3. The one and only medium through which the Spirit works is the Scriptures; therefore, we "reason out of the Scriptures" like Paul did.

4. These preceding principles give us the true motivation for evangelism—a zeal for God and a love for others.

5. There is a constant danger of heresy through a false zeal and employment of unscriptural methods.[4]

I have begun this examination of evangelism by describing the idea of witness. Now let's shift to a scriptural study of what constitutes the "whole gospel." We'll do this both negatively (by way of contrast with a partial gospel) and positively (by way of presenting an outline and commentary on the central elements of the gospel).

2
The Gospel Reduced

What is the difference between these two statements?

"The minimum amount of truth to the maximum number of people."

"The maximum amount of truth to the maximum number of people."

Only two words: Minimum, maximum. But those words constitute a difference as great as night and day. The first statement unfortunately seems to summarize the goal of much contemporary evangelism. The second describes the historic and biblical goal in evangelism.

Packaging the Gospel
The first statement typifies how many look at our evangelistic task. The evangelism professor I described earlier exemplifies this approach. Yes, he is an extreme example. Nevertheless, he has

merely taken to a logical conclusion the assumptions that undergird the majority of today's evangelistic training materials, seminars and speakers. So often we are told to think of the gospel content in terms of a simple plan of salvation with three or four basic facts. Yet the mandate our Lord gave us was "teaching them to obey everything I have commanded you" (Mt. 28:20). In another version of this command we find what we are witnesses to: the Christ, the necessity of his suffering, the historical resurrection, repentance, forgiveness of sins (Lk. 24:46-48). Precisely so, comments the modern evangelist, we are only to repeat a few central facts, for Paul himself summarizes the gospel ever so briefly (1 Cor. 15:3-4) and explicitly tells us in the second chapter of the same book that he "resolved to know nothing while I was with you except Jesus Christ and him crucified" (v. 2). Likewise, many of today's evangelists continue trying to prove their case for stripping down the complicated theology of the gospel to a minimal amount of truth content. While they no doubt are sincerely seeking to help others toward salvation, they can end up dangerously misleading people by making the gospel simplistic.

Is this simple gospel approach adequate? Are we to reduce and package the gospel for easy distribution? Are we to imagine that Paul merely parroted the words, "Jesus Christ crucified," up and down the streets of Corinth? No. Each of these words is like the tip of an iceberg rising above the water. Underneath is a large mass of assumptions and deep meanings. Only when we grapple with these can we begin to understand the nature and breadth of our evangelistic task. This is why in the book of Acts we see the apostles as *teachers*—reasoning, persuading, explaining—involved in all sorts of teaching activity in order to communicate as much truth as possible to nonbelievers.[1]

J. I. Packer in *Evangelism and the Sovereignty of God* has pointed out that the gospel was a message of some complexity, needing to be learned before it could be lived by and understood before it could be applied. It needed, therefore, to be taught. The first and fundamental job of Paul as a preacher of the gospel was to communicate knowledge, to get truth fixed in people's minds. Teaching the truth was the basic evangelistic activity.[2] Although the apostles as evangelists did keep certain themes in the forefront, these central doctrines could never be communicated in a vacuum. They must be related to the whole counsel of God. There must be a context given to the points of the gospel or else communication cannot take place. We must allow, however, for a great difference between what a Christian's understanding of the gospel should be and that of a non-Christian who is just beginning to learn it. For Paul, the only right method of evangelism was the teaching method. Therefore, Scriptural evangelism has extensive—not minimal—instruction as its goal.

In place of this scriptural stance, since about 1900, a new method of packaging the gospel has now come into evangelicalism.[3] We are to make the gospel readily transferable so as to gain the mental assent of the hearer. This has led to the idea of "the simple gospel," which we all supposedly know as soon as we become Christians. But this approach encourages us to think of the gospel as a pill that will cure all. We, as doctors, dispense it freely. We need not worry about the patient's symptoms. No matter what the symptom is, the pill will cure it. Thus, many of us abridge our analysis of the disease (sin), instead of taking time to expose the person's *sinful* nature which creates the sickness. Our object has become merely to convince people to take the cure. They do not need to know the problem—just the answer. Such treatment, however, makes the gospel vulnerable to being molded by the carnal desires of the sinner or the fads of the secular world (Jesus as revolutionary, liberator of the oppressed, movie star, and so on).

If we carry through with the logic of simplistic evangelism, we need not discuss gospel content. Our evangelism training is directed toward *mobilizing quickly* (enter population growth statistics and world-to-end-soon-prophets) *everyone* (no matter what doctrines of the gospel he or she holds). This large scale unity of Christians for evangelism is on the basis of a common need to get the job done and a vague belief in the conversion experience.

Have you ever noticed that most conferences on evangelism concentrate on methods not on the message content? This methodological emphasis is not the property of one denomination, mission or organization alone. It has become a hallmark of the evangelical subculture. Most Christians growing up in this century, reading only post-1900 popular Christian literature, have unconsciously imbibed this "methodism" along with its truncated gospel posing as the whole gospel.

The person who has known only vanilla ice cream might look on cherry vanilla with suspicion at first. My plea is that we taste and see the difference between modern evangelism with its man-centered gospel and the historic God-centered gospel. We should not be oblivious to the clear teaching of Scripture nor ignorant of the teaching of those people of God who stand in the stream of historic Christianity in ages before our own. Man-centered evangelism shortens the message. It so focuses on man that it reduces God. It so fears further doctrinal division among true Christians that it allows the most imprecise gospel messages to become common currency.[4] The method-centered approach views the Bible as a mere source of "evangelistic texts," rather than as a book whose total focus is Christ. But in reality the entire Scripture can be used in evangelism because it is entirely about Christ.

To obtain a clear view of the whole gospel we must first cut away the sprawling undergrowth of a man-centered emphasis.

What then is method- or man-centered evangelism? How does it differ from God-centered evangelism? Let me begin my definition by first contrasting them in some aspects of the content of the gospel that each emphasizes. Later (at the end of part three) we will see how their views of gospel content influence our practices in witnessing.

Since salvation benefits us, there is not a complete antithesis between the two views. We are helped, loved and rewarded in God's gospel. God centers his designs on saving people. When reading Table 1 many will find themselves somewhere in between the two views. If the chart stimulates you to re-examine your evan-

Table 1/Some Contrasts in Gospel Content

Man-centered	God-centered
View of God	
Point of contact with non-Christians is love (God loves you). Therefore, God's authority is secondary.	Point of contact with non-Christians is creation (God made you). Therefore, God has authority over your destiny.
Love is God's chief attribute.	Holiness and love are equally important attributes of God.
God is impotent before the sinner's will.	God is able to empower the sinner's will.
The persons of the Trinity have different goals in accomplishing and applying salvation.	The persons of the Trinity work in harmony—salvation accomplished for and applied to the same people.
God is a friend who will help you.	*God is a king who will save you.*
View of Humanity	
Fallen, yet has the ability (or potential) to choose the good.	Fallen, and will not come to God by own will power.
Seeks truth but lacks correct facts.	Mind at enmity with God; none seek God.
Needs love, help, friendship.	Needs new nature (mind, heart, will), regeneration.
Makes mistakes, is imperfect, needs forgiveness.	Rebels against God, has a sinful nature, needs reconciliation.
Needs salvation from the consequences of sin—unhappiness, hell.	Needs salvation from guilt and the power of sin.
Humanity is sick and ignorant.	*Humanity is dead and lost.*
View of Christ	
Savior from selfishness, mistakes, hell.	Savior from sin and sinful nature.
He exists for our benefit.	He exists to gather a kingdom and receive honor and glory.
His death was more important than his life.	His death and his life of obedience equally important.
Emphasizes his priestly office—Savior.	Emphasizes his priestly, kingly, and prophetic offices.
An attitude of submission to Christ's lordship is optional for salvation.	*An attitude of submission to Christ's lordship is necessary for salvation.*

View of Response to Christ

Invitation waiting to be accepted now.	Loving command to be obeyed now.
Our choice is the basis for salvation—God responds to our decision.	God's choice is the basis for salvation—we respond to God's initiative.
We give mental assent to truths of gospel—decision.	We respond with our whole person (mind, heart, will)—conversion.
Appeal is made to the desires of the sinner.	Truths are driven home into the conscience of the sinner.
Saved by faith alone—repentance omitted for it is thought of as "works."	Saved by faith alone—saving faith always accompanied by repentance.
Assurance of salvation comes from a counselor using the promises of God and pronouncing the new believer saved.	Assurance of salvation comes from the Holy Spirit applying biblical promises to the conscience and effecting a changed life.
Sinners have the key in their hands.	*God has the key in his hand.*

gelistic message, it has achieved its purpose. The point is that our theology really does shape our methodology.

I want now to elaborate on what seems to me a big difference between biblical evangelism and modern evangelism. It can be summarized in three ways: a whole gospel versus a truncated gospel; a message-centered gospel versus a method-centered gospel; a God-centered gospel versus a man-centered gospel.

Whole Gospel/Truncated Gospel

How dangerous a half-truth can be when presented as the whole truth! For instance, the truth that God loves sinners is a wonderful part of the gospel. However, if the whole presentation of the gospel rests on this truth, distortion develops. Sinners can relax with the thought of God's love for them and find an excuse to delay repentance. This biblical truth can also be easily interpreted by non-Christians to mean, "Love is God." That is, a human definition of love is substituted and sinners find great comfort in the fact that such love personified will never hurt them or judge them. A biblical truth thus becomes twisted into an excuse for complacency.

But what if the truth that God is love were balanced with God is light? God is pure, holy, perfect. He is angry with sin and will punish those who persist in it. The love of God now is given a backbone. It is seen as a tough love not as sentimentalism. That he can still love sinners and freely offer himself to all who believe becomes astounding news. One good question to evaluate any gospel presentation of God is, "Was the nature of God defined clearly?"

Another example of a half-truth found in much gospel literature is this: "To become a Christian is to become happy, fulfilled, and to live an adventurous and exciting life." But what about the other side of the coin? In evangelism we should also mention the suffering and cost of discipleship.

Perhaps reading for yourself an example of some evangelistic literature will help you see my point. Here is a pamphlet consisting mostly of Scripture. What do you think of the title, the ending and the overall thrust?

Meet My Friend
He is faithful.
"When my father and my mother forsake me, then the Lord will take me up" (Psalm 27:10).
    He is the way to God the Father.
"Jesus saith . . . I am the Way, the Truth, and the Life: no man cometh unto the Father but by Me" (John 14:6).
    He already loves you.
"But God commendeth His love toward us, in that, while we were yet sinners,* Christ died for us" (Romans 5:8).
*"For all have sinned and come short of the glory of God" (Romans 3:23).
    He wants to give you eternal life.
"Believe on the Lord Jesus Christ, and thou shalt be saved" (Acts 16:31). "For God so loved the world, that He gave His only begotten Son, that whosoever believeth in Him should not perish, but have everlasting life" (John 3:16).
    He is the only one who can give you eternal life.

"Neither is there salvation in any other: for there is none other name under heaven given among men, whereby we must be saved" (Acts 4:12).

He won't refuse anyone.

"Him that cometh to Me I will in no wise cast out" (John 6:37).

Now that you have met my Friend, don't you feel that you want to commit your life for time and for eternity into His hands? Right now you can take the Lord Jesus Christ as your own personal Saviour and Friend.[5]

A lack of understanding the doctrines of the gospel can mislead the sinner *and* the saint in their duties. The sinner isn't sure of the proper response, and the saint isn't sure of the correct message. Many of our gospel tracts and much of our evangelistic training, if not in actual error, are woefully lacking in helping us define precisely who God is, who we are and what sin is. Well-meaning Christians have adopted easy formulas leading into an easy-believism. A renowned preacher in the Alliance Church, A. W. Tozer, comments, "All unannounced and mostly undetected there has come in modern times a new cross into popular evangelical circles. It is like the old cross, but different: the likenesses are superficial; the differences are fundamental. . . . This new evangelism employs the same language as the old, but its content is not the same and its emphasis is not as before."[6] Without judging motives, let us call one another to renewed study of the whole counsel of God.

Message-centered/Method-centered

What is method-centered witness? Peruse the content of most seminars on evangelism and compare the proportion of material given to the gospel message with that given to methodology. Consider the practice of singing many songs coupled with long and urgent appeals at the end of an evangelistic service. Such methods are validated with the argument that "a decision from the non-Christian must be evoked." Have you ever urged someone to "try God"? There is a whole method of evangelism based on this idea of experimenting for one week. You pray and put God to the test—try him out for a while and see if he doesn't work better than anything else you've tried.

In the new evangelism, doctrinal content is slighted and the emphasis falls on methods of selling the gospel to people. Often this takes the form of recommending that a non-Christian duplicate another's conversion experience. However, Scripture declares the priority of truth over experience. The thrust of the Bible asks us to conform our experience to revealed truth, not to start with our experience (no matter how beautiful or helpful it may have been to us) and then make a doctrine for others from it. The model for our witness is not to be a smooth-talking public relations agent but an ambassador with a proclamation from a King.

Doctrine and life, truth and the practice of that truth have been joined together by God. Our message will mold our evangelistic methods and regulate our spiritual experiences. We must not use an incongruous medium to present the God of truth. Modern electronic media (radio, TV, film, computers, multimedia and so on) have great potential for evangelism if they preserve theological content and avoid manipulation.

By knowing truth, we will be set free. It is by the force of gospel truths alone that people are to be led to seek Christ and not by our reliance on either the latest persuasion techniques from the business world or the newest psychological tricks dished out through paperback publishers. We are not to try to entice people by methods appealing to their desires. It is wrong to key into the non-Christian's interests by saying the gospel offers the same thing as the world does. Tozer points out that whatever the sin-mad world happens to be clamoring after at the moment is cleverly shown to be the very thing the new gospel offers, only religion's product is better.

I have found two questions helpful to guard against this aberration. "Was enough of the gospel taught to make an appeal for response meaningful? Was the conscience probed, or only our natural desires addressed?"

Take a look at this tract which was written to lead a person to Christ, and see what you think.

What Is Your Favorite Game?
Playing games is a common pastime, whether you realize it or not. Not checkers or dominoes or chess, but social games which we devise to make us feel closer to other people.

One girl turns on her radio every night just in time to hear the announcer say, "And now we bid you a very pleasant good night." It is a human voice speaking to her.

A grandmother goes shopping and buys another unneeded hat. She is disappointed because her husband has been called out of town again. So she is off to grab a new thing to try to cure that empty feeling.

One woman calls another to have lunch. They sip their coffee and talk all around themselves; but they never really make contact.

A bachelor plays house with an eager co-ed he has met. He wants someone in his apartment to talk with.

What is it that we hunt for in life? What do we really want? What moves us through day after day, month after month, year after year?

Our needs are many. We cry "gimme" by our attitudes, our glances, our conversation, our actions. We find many stopgap answers, but always there is the big hole, begging to be filled. We pour into it an astonishing collection of things: work projects, television, athletics, clubs, travel, entertainment, volunteer service, parties, barbiturates. But if we are honest, we have to admit that the human satisfaction we gain creates a longing for even greater fulfillment than anything we have yet experienced. The deepest want of all is to find what some people call an "at-oneness." Some call it "peace of soul" or "peace with God."

The truth about our human involvements is that they both meet and do not meet our deepest needs. Life is spent in an effort to overcome the separation that is common to persons everywhere. The expectation of really belonging to someone drives us on in constant search. We know the superb moment of discovery as we find a kindred spirit. But we also know the dawning realization that even this special person is not enough!

There is no substitute for knowing God. He made us in His own image, and our reunion with Him is the foundation for everything else we seek. There is no relationship or game serious enough to satisfy our restless search for completeness. The only way to realize satisfaction and fulfillment is to say "yes" to God, who is love. When we say "no" to His will, we are not only out of place with Him but out of relationship with our fellowman.

People have been trying to bridge their separate existences since the world began. But God has already stepped over the gulf. Christ Jesus came to our world in a human form we can understand. He came as a servant, to say yes to everything God asked of Him. He became obedient to the death of the cross so that we might be saved from our isolation.

If all this is true, then you are wasting your time playing games to win satisfaction. Consider saying "yes" to Jesus Christ, because that's what you were made for. And you won't ever be satisfied until you are "at one" with Jesus Christ.[7]

God-centered/Man-centered

Man-centered evangelism contains some biblical truths. Yet these are distorted, for error comes when truth is given out of context. Allen Harris has described the effects of centering on man as three-fold:

1. Deceiving non-Christians—unbelievers trust in their "response" for assurance.

2. Distorting Christians—believers looking for another stage in their Christian life, often becoming disillusioned.

3. Disgracing God's honor—people professing salvation with unchanged lives.

Most of us probably fall somewhere between being God-centered and man-centered evangelists. May God help us not to contradict the character of God in our witnessing. May the God to whom we witness be consistent with the God we worship. Our evangelism needs to stress a God of holiness whom we worship—not just a God who exists to give us good times and pleasant feelings. We gained redemption through a sovereign Savior rather than through a relationship to him as a mere friend. The life of a Christian is to be radically different from, not relatively similar to, the world.

Man-centered evangelism is not radical enough in its opposition to sinful human nature. Tozer again helps us see this, calling it "the new cross."

The new cross does not slay the sinner; it redirects him. It gears him into a cleaner and jollier way of living and saves his self-respect. To the self assertive it says, "Come and assert yourself for Christ." To the egotist it says, "Come and do your boasting in the Lord." To the thrill-seeker it says, "Come and enjoy the thrill of the abundant Christian life." The idea behind this kind of thing may be sincere, but its sincerity does not save it from being false. It misses completely the whole meaning of the cross. The cross is a symbol of death. It stands for the abrupt, violent end of a person. God salvages the individual by liquidating him and then raising him to newness of life. The corn of wheat must fall into the ground and die. God then bestows life, but not an improved old life. Whoever would possess it must pass under the rod. He must repudiate himself and concur in God's just sentence against him. How can this theology be translated in life? Simply, the non-Christian must repent and believe. He must forsake his sins and then go on to forsake himself. Let him cover nothing, defend nothing, excuse nothing. Let him not seek to make terms with God, but let him bow his head before the stroke of God's stern displeasure and acknowledge himself worthy to die.[8]

In light of Tozer's words, what do you think of this next tract?

You're a Beautiful Person

But—even beautiful people have problems. Problems like Life (?) Sin (?) Eternity (?) God (?) God (?) (!) What's He got to do with it? Everything, Like, try this—

Jesus Christ said:

As it is written, There is none righteous, no, not one.

I am the way, the truth, and the life; no man cometh unto the Father, but by me.

I am the light of the world; he that followeth me shall not walk in darkness, but shall have the light of life.

I am the door; by me if any man enter in, he shall be saved.

He that believeth on him is not condemned; but he that believeth not is condemned already, because he hath not believed in the name of the only begotten Son of God.

Sound Strong? Hang on!

I gave you this because I believe it is the most important message in the world.

God loves you, no matter who you are or what you are. He sent His Son, Jesus Christ, to die as payment for your sins. That's love! But Christ not only died for you, He arose from the dead and now lives! Jesus Christ is a living Saviour. He lives to give you real joy, real peace, and an eternal hope.

Now, how can you know this Christ as your personal Saviour?

Well, Christ said, "Behold, I stand at the door, and knock; if any man hear my voice, and open the door, I will come in to him."

Receiving Christ involves completely giving yourself to God, trusting Christ to forgive your sins, and allowing Him to have control of your life. The Bible says, "Whosoever shall call on the name of the Lord shall be saved."

Listen! Now is the time for you to accept Christ as your SAVIOUR! Don't put it off. God warns in His Word, "Now is the accepted time; behold, now is the day of salvation."[9]

Is the Ogre Really There?

In a God-centered gospel, grace is central. God is exalted at every point in the outworking of it—from its design in all eternity through its outworking in Christ and its application to his people. Our King is assured of a kingdom and will neither be frustrated by human resistance nor obligated to save his creatures because of their supposed rights to his favor. We rejoice in the benefits that accrue to all of us from a gracious God, but we glory in our God alone and the vindication of his honor above whatever good may come to humanity.

Some may say the ogre of man-centered evangelism is not as prevalent as I have indicated. I say it is. We have only to look into the ghetto of the evangelical church to find it. We can also look at our own hearts and evangelistic practice and find how woefully inconsistent we all are. I have sharply drawn the contrast between these two approaches in evangelism. Yes, there is some caricaturization. A great amount of evangelism falls between these opposing perspectives. Yet just as a drawn caricature of a famous person has just enough resemblance in it to be recognizable, so I hope the points in my caricature of evangelism are useful in clarifying the substantive issues.

3
The Gospel Recovered

It is one thing to be painfully aware of weaknesses in evangelistic messages and attempt to evaluate them. It is another thing
to try to put forward a positive example of the direction in which
we must head. With all the abuses in simplistic gospel approaches,
we must be careful not to rule out attempts to elucidate clearly
the main elements of the gospel. It is a temptation to be only crit-
ical and not to try honestly, humbly and lovingly to build toward a
remedy.

Gospel Roots
I have a vivid recollection of reading through the entire book of
Acts in one sitting with some friends. Ernie, a friend from church
during my college days, took a half-dozen students one Saturday
out into the woods and hills of central Pennsylvania. We did a survey of Acts, looking for the content of the gospel proclaimed by

the early church. I never forgot what I read of the evangelistic message of those early believers. Their approach, like that of Jesus, was never stereotyped. It was theological and personal.

In studying Acts we discover that the evangelists brought out certain gospel truths again and again. Their witness was also versatile. They were aware of unbelievers as individuals in unique situations. Yet, there was a basic grid or "pattern of sound words" that proved a useful springboard for the memories of evangelists. It kept them on the track. They turned again and again to the pivotal points of the gospel. It was not, however, a straitjacket, inhibiting all imagination and initiative on their part.[1]

The outline in Table 2 is not perfect, but it is an attempt to fix in our mind certain poles around which truths cluster so that we will have a clear understanding when we talk with nonbelievers. Any attitude of "now I have it" betrays ignorance and pride. Likewise, an attitude of "holding back" in my witnessing until I "comprehend" the gospel is sinful.

Often, along with the idea of learning such an outline comes the concept that there are many people just waiting to hear these several hundred words and anxious to believe. This assumption is not generally true. There are exceptions, as we find people quickly converted in the New Testament (such as the thief on the cross or the Philippian jailer), but these people were under conviction of sin and prepared by God's Spirit.

We must not make the mistake of thinking that people are converted because they follow our line of reasoning as we explain the gospel. It may be helpful for nonbelievers to see the overall picture, but they may be far from any sense of awe of God as Creator, conviction of personal sin and hunger for redemption.

On the other hand, it is certainly helpful for believers to have a framework on which to begin to build a more systematic comprehension of our great salvation. Any such outline should be filled in by thorough meditation in the Scriptures, personal communion with Jehovah, and active listening to solid preaching that exposits and applies the Word. It will help to memorize the central points of the outline, whether it is this one, or one you develop yourself.[2]

More will be said in part three about the proper use of an outline. Passages as well as key verses have been noted in the outline as an aid to teaching these truths more fully and in context. Verses from both the Old and New Testaments are used to show the unity of revelation and as an aid for talking with Jews. I am indebted to Allen Harris for the framework of the outline in Table 2.

Gospel Grammar: An Explanation of Salient Points in the Outline
I. God—the Holy and Loving Creator
It is instructive to compare Paul's evangelism among the Jews with his evangelism among the Gentiles.[3] When he was speaking in the synagogue (Acts 13:16-42), he knew his audience had a good foundation on which to build. He could assume a certain world view. He knew that terms like *God* and *sin* would communicate accurately because his hearers, steeped in Old Testament revelation, packed the right content into the words.

Far too many Christians today are making this assumption about their hearers—not that they think most people are Jewish but they think that our audience understands some basic concepts in the Bible. Although most Western countries have a Christian historical background, the dominant world views of average people are not Christian at all. Even if our audience is Jewish, most of them have imbibed a relativistic world view and are ignorant of the real meaning of many biblical words.

What purports to be the most modern and up-to-date evangelism is, in fact, outdated at this point. Such evangelists rattle off "God words" like *eternal life, holy, salvation* and *sin,* fling truth at people, and then ask their hearers to "decide" for a contentless Christ. Any such decision amounts to a leap in the dark. It opts for solutions to surface problems by means of a religion trip. We must always be careful not to assume too much on the part of our hearers, even though they may use the same words that we do. For the few outspoken atheists we meet, we will encounter droves of people who use biblical words to which they attach their own definitions.

I remember being in Ft. Lauderdale one year at the time of spring break for many college students. I used two questions with a number of them, as I ambled from person to person on that sunny beach. "Do you believe in God?" Most replied, "Yes." Then I asked, "Does sin separate you from God?" Their replies were brief, but astounding. "No, why should it?" or "I don't believe in that kind of a God," or "My concept of God is one who loves." How many times have each of us talked to someone who does not balk at the word *God,* and may profess to believe in him, yet defines God out of personal ideas and values?

The concept we want to drive home, highlighted under "Main Point" in the outline, is God's ownership of each of us. An individual must be brought to see that he is not the master of his fate nor the captain of his soul. In the words of a James Ward song, "I must be brought down, all the way down—till I come to you with my face on the ground." What does this ownership mean?

In the ancient Middle East there existed suzerains—sovereign monarchs of a land. These rulers held absolute sway over their subjects. It was a suzerain's prerogative to initiate a treaty with his subjects. This was no bilateral agreement negotiated between two equal parties; rather, it was a sovereignly imposed law. He bound his subjects to himself, in effect owning them. In return, not because he was in any way obligated to but purely out of his self-determined will, he pledged himself to protect, defend and show mercy to his subjects. If they kept covenant with their suzerain king, all was well—they would experience blessing from his mercy. If they broke covenant, they would be liable to his righteous indignation, his terrible curse. God is our suzerain king.

Now let's look at how Paul emphasizes God's ownership as he moves among the Gentiles. When he enters the pagan marketplace (Acts 17:22-34; see also Acts 14:11-18), he begins to amplify his proclamation into a work of teaching because he was concerned to *communicate.* He was not trying to intellectualize the

Table 2/An Introductory Outline of a God-centered Gospel: God as Creator and Redeemer

I God—the Holy and Loving Creator

A *Sovereign Creator:* Out of his pleasure and freedom God created and sustains us. Therefore, we are utterly dependent upon him for everything we have. We have no inherent rights. God is *light,* which symbolizes his majesty, purity and holiness. He sets the standard of right and wrong. He is God Almighty in heaven over his creation.

B *Personal Creator:* We are neither impersonal machines nor animals. Our significance is derived from our unique creation in the image of the God who is a person. God is *love,* and made us for the purpose of communion with him—to worship and honor him, and to fellowship with and delight in him. He is God, the Father of us his creatures.

Main Point: God has an absolute claim on our lives as our Creator. We are responsible to reflect God.

Key Verses: Psalm 100:3; Matthew 5:48

Key Passages: Exodus 19:16-20; 20:1-26; Matthew 5:17-48; Acts 17:24-31

Question:

Since God's wonderful character, his rights as Creator, his blessings and his warnings are all designed to remind us of his loving ownership of us, why don't we love him with all our heart, soul, mind and strength?

Diagram:

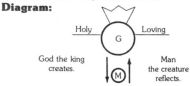

Holy — G — Loving

God the king creates.　　Man the creature reflects.

II Man—the Sinful Creature

A *Definition of Sin:* Willful rebellion by refusing to do what God commands; determining to do what he forbids. We find ourselves:

1 Playing God: running our lives as if God did not matter; ignoring God; trying to be self-sufficient and self-made people.

2 Fighting God: violating and disregarding his Law for living; wanting to decide for ourselves what is right and wrong.

B *Consequences of Sin:* Death (separation). Both physical and spiritual death due to the wrath of God.

1 Living Death: Separation now from God resulting in guilt, loss of identity, purposelessness, distorted relationships and so on.

2 Eternal Death: Separation of our souls from God forever. Hell is real.

Main Point: We are self-deceived if we think we are living out of our own resources, when actually we are creatures and guilty rebels under judgment who cannot help ourselves. We have chosen to reject God.

Key Verses: Jeremiah 17:9; Romans 3:20; James 2:10

Key Passages: Isaiah 64:6-7; Romans 1:20-25; 3:10-20; 7:7-13; Philippians 3:4-6

Question:

Why do we deny responsibility for our sins and continue to live with guilt?

Diagram:

God's judgment is upon those who sin by trying to play God.　　Our sin blocks the way and separates us from God.

III Christ—the Merciful Redeemer

A *Teacher:* Christ's words and life reveal the nature of God. He communicates to our conscience, and we submit to his authority in Scripture.

B *Sin-bearer:* He offered himself as the innocent, substitutionary sacrifice for sin on behalf of all who acknowledge their sin. He took the guilt of sinners upon himself and endured God's judgment for it in his death on the cross. He redeems them by his blood poured out, which satisfies the just anger of a holy God against sinful people.

C *King:* He rose from the dead (conquered sin and death) and ascended back to his Father to be Lord. His life of perfect obedience is now vindicated and he freely and sovereignly gives his reward of righteousness to undeserving sinners. He dispenses grace (unmerited favor) to whomever he will and rules, in love, over all united to him.

Main Point: Jesus as the God-man is the only way to life—by his life, death and resurrection as Redeemer.

Key Verses: Isaiah 53:5; Mark 10:45; Ephesians 1:7

Key Passages: Isaiah 53:1-11; 43:25; Mark 10:33-34, 45; Acts 2:22-24, 36

Question: **Diagram:**

How does Christ's death on the cross display both the holiness and love of God?

 We are forgiven because Christ on the cross bore God's judgment.

 God in Christ redeems sinful people.

IV Our Necessary Response to Be United to Christ

On the basis of these historical truths, and because Christ is alive today, God invites and commands us now to:

A *Turn* from our rebellion to Christ as Lord with our whole selves in our:

1 *Minds:* Agree with God that we have wronged him and deserve his judgment. Realize that his goodness shown to us in many ways was designed to humble us unto repentance.

2 *Emotions:* Despise our sins and our sinful nature.

3 *Wills:* Determine to turn from our rebellion and serve our Creator and Redeemer. See Christ alone as the payer for and the power over our sin.

Key Verse: Isaiah 55:7

Key Passages: Isaiah 12:1-3; 1 Thessalonians 1:9-10

B *Trust* in nothing that we can do, but only in the finished work of Christ as Savior with our:

1 *Minds:* Recognize Christ as the necessary and sufficient payment for sin.

2 *Emotions:* Long for Christ and rejoice in his love for the undeserving.

3 *Wills:* Commit our lives to Christ by casting ourselves upon him as our only hope for reconciliation with God. Transfer our trust from ourselves to him. Take for ourselves his gift of forgiveness and righteousness. Ask for God's mercy.

Key Verse: John 1:12   **Key Passages:** Romans 3:21-26; John 3:16-18

Main Point: A person can only become a Christian by turning from a sinful life to Christ and by trusting in him as Savior and Lord. There is a cost to becoming a disciple of Jesus. Read Mark 8:34-38 and Luke 14:25-33. Ask the Holy Spirit to enable you to turn and trust.

Conclusion: Read Psalm 51:1-17; Isaiah 53:1-11; Galatians 2:20 and pray to God for his help. When he answers you, tell someone and seek out the friendship of Christians who take the Bible seriously.

gospel for certain audiences. Anyone who makes the gospel sophisticated and abstract is not making a New Testament proclamation but is trusting in human understanding and his own wisdom (1 Cor. 2:4-5). It is precisely because Paul knew the crude polytheism of his audience (note how observant he was even as he entered the city) that he is careful to delineate the true God from his hearers' false religious notions. As mysticism and pantheism become an increasing part of the syncretism in religions around us, we must carefully distinguish the biblical God by patiently instructing others in his nature.

In Acts 17 Paul teaches the basics about the nature of God. The Lord is transcendent and immanent. He controls history and our destiny. He has a purpose for humanity. He is the Creator; we are his creatures. Paul first fixes his definition of God by positives and then negatives, teaching antithetically. He emphasizes to the conscience of his audience the difference between their concepts of God and the world and the biblical view.[4] God is personal (pronoun *he*). He is holy ("will judge by righteousness"). He requires repentance and obedience to his authority ("commands"). History has a goal! ("he has set a day"). Christ is the resurrected mediator of all judgment (v. 31).

It is absolutely amazing how much instruction is given about who God is in this summary of a powerful evangelistic sermon. Here's a content-filled gospel message that can be the basis for the conversation with a philosopher or a child. I know; I've used it effectively with both.

Luke tells us we are to witness to the necessity of Christ's sufferings (Lk. 24:46-48). How can we do this without going into the nature of God's character as *holy* and *loving?* These two attributes sum up God's moral character, and form the motive and shape the means of God's plan of salvation. We cannot explain the work of Christ unless we present a true picture of God.

We must give people a thorough grounding in the character of God as the self-sufficient *Creator* as part of our basic gospel. The theory of evolution is uncritically assumed by the college student and the ghetto grandmother. We preach the gospel in a space age in which all people sense their finitude to a new degree, and see technology as the creator and sustainer of life. We are insignificant, and only animals at that—this is the common attitude. The erosion in the Western world of the Creator-creature distinction, which is foundational to all biblical thought, constitutes a serious challenge to our evangelism. The absence of this crucial distinction forms a barrier to unbelievers seeing their responsibility before their Maker. We must work very hard to communicate that people are responsible for their actions and that these will be evaluated.

When we speak to people who have no foundational concepts about the true Creator God, let us be thankful God has spoken and defined himself. Most of my time in witnessing is taken up with defining the nature of the biblical God. We now find joy in witnessing; and with God's definitions on our lips, we reinforce the "law written in the heart" (Rom. 2:15), that God-implanted sensor. As we witness we touch that light-sensitive nerve deep in the heart of nonbelievers with the hot iron of revelatory truth.

II. Man—the Sinful Creature

Sin and *God* are correlative terms. If you deny God, you are also denying the existence of sins. If the biblical God exists, then it follows that he must disapprove and take action against much that is common in today's world. By reminding people who God is, we show them who they are—both in terms of their significance and in the horror of their sinfulness. The human individual is noble, a special creation of God, built to reflect God's moral characteristics. Yet the same individual is also horribly ignoble, spoiled by the Fall and the spoiler of all creation. The corruption of what is best will lead to the worst results. This incongruity between our nobility and our ignobility is revealed in every newspaper. A human interest story tells how the people of the neighborhood have pooled their resources to help a child cruelly crippled in an accident. Two pages later a story reveals that some of the same people are shunning a South Vietnamese family "because they're different." How can human beings be so inconsistent? At one time they display self-sacrifice, and the next moment they are all selfishness and pride. This creates a point of tension that we have a responsibility to press onto those we talk with. When people are able to accept the fact of the human condition, they will be better able to see who they are. Man plays God and man fights God.

The gospel challenges each of us with the question, What is man? The naked ape or the genetic freak? The chemical machine or the quirk of chance? We must help people to personalize the theories they hold in order to see if they are practicable. We need to get them to answer the question "Who am I?" in terms of the logic of their own position. If they finally admit, for example, that being a naturalist means they believe people are quirks of chance or complex machines, then we can bring them back into God's world and cry with them as they long for relationships, love, communication, personality. These gifts are from God to show human beings they are significant. But the world view of most non-Christians will not allow them to have these gifts.

In all our emphasis on teaching the truth of the whole gospel, we would be denying part of this gospel if we were not listening and being sensitive to the person we face. If we don't treat people as *persons* when we witness to them, we deny a basic tenet of the very gospel we say we believe in. If we turn this outline into a formula, we have depersonalized those we encounter. We can be blunt about the hard subject of sin with a person, if at the same time we treat that person as a unique individual.

In explaining what it means to be human, we must vividly contrast Genesis 2 and 3 (creation and Fall) and personally punctuate Romans 1:18-23 (creature tries to be the Creator). That is, from these scriptures people should be shown what they were made to be, and then discover what they have instead become. As soon as we talk about man, therefore, we of necessity talk about sin.

Sin is a term like the word *God* that is part of common conversation. To most, it means dramatic wrongs done to others—rape, embezzlement, killing, child battering. Well and good, but people who think of sin only in these categories (dramatics and horizontal relationships) will have a difficult time seeing why *they* need Christ. Other people might—because they are the "real sinners." But to admit I am sinful in my *nature* (not just that I make mistakes or am imperfect), and by simply not loving God I have offended his holiness, making me liable to punishment—this is a concept of sin totally foreign and distasteful to our minds.

Since everybody's life includes acts and attitudes that cause dissatisfaction and shame, everyone has a bad conscience about something.

> The danger is that in our evangelism we should content ourselves with evoking thoughts of these things and making people feel uncomfortable about them, and then depicting Christ as the One who saves us from these elements of ourselves, without even raising the question of our relationship with God. Unless we see our shortcomings in the light of the law and holiness of God, we do not see them *as sin* at all. For sin is not a social concept; it is a theological concept. To preach sin is not to make capital out of peoples' felt frailties (the brainwasher's trick), but to measure their lives by the holy law of God. To be convicted of sin means not just to feel one is an all-around flop but to realize that one has offended God.[5]

If you now think that we're stumped in our evangelism unless we can obtain a confession of hideous misdeeds and thoughts from non-Christians, let me explain. We do not only try to expose peoples' weaknesses, but in addition we show them their strengths. We acknowledge the fine qualities that they may have. These are areas of their lives in which they consider themselves to be self-sufficient and secure. We point out that such a thought is in fact evidence of the depth of their depravity. People need to discover their strengths are gifts from God. They have experienced God's goodness that is designed to bring them to humility, thankfulness and repentance (Rom. 2:4).

Many people have a naturally bad conscience from a sense of mistakes, imperfection and inability to live up to their own standards. We must guard against equating this conscience with a spiritual conviction of sin. Packer points out that true conviction of sin includes:

1. Awareness of a wrong relationship with *God*—not just with self or others, or a general sense of need, but a specific need of reconciliation with God.

2. Conviction of *sins*—a sense of guilt for particular wrongs.

3. Conviction of *sinfulness*—a sense of helplessness to do right and consequent need of a new heart or rebirth. Any goodness I claim is not inherent but derived from God. Our righteousness is not good enough, either quantitatively or qualitatively.[6]

So let us not fail to impress upon sinners the basic truth about their condition before a holy God. Yet, we are *not* in the business of judging too closely the amount of conviction needed before a person is ready to receive Christ. Good evangelists are doctors who use the surgical knife of the law summarized in the Ten Commandments and elaborated in the Sermon on the Mount to expose the sinful character of sin. By our comprehensive teaching of such passages from Scripture, we free the religious Sauls of our day by exposing them to the high standard of God's law, even though the commandment may slay them at first. Repetition and perseverance are important here. It was not until the tenth commandment that the moral young man (Lk. 18:18-30) and Saul recognized their sin. "Indeed I would not have known what sin was except through the law. For I would not have known what it was to covet if the law had not said, 'Do not covet' " (Rom. 7:7).

What if a surgeon were in the midst of a lifesaving operation and discovered his scalpel was missing? In anguish he would complain, "I don't have the right instrument for this incision!"

We too have been called on to be doctors—physicians of the soul. We've been given a scalpel, and yet at times we've failed to use it. However, it is of absolute necessity for our operation on the hearts of nonbelievers. This scalpel has never failed, no matter whose hand held it. It has always accomplished its purpose. Its edge is so sharp it can cut between thoughts and intentions of the heart. Of course, I'm speaking of the scalpel of the Scriptures. It compels *conviction* of sin and reveals a *compassionate* Savior— guilt (law) and forgiveness (love). Although all of Scripture carries this double message, there are some passages that make especially keen scalpels. Repentance toward God and faith in the Lord Jesus Christ (Acts 20:21) is the goal of the gospel, so let us examine in turn the use of law and love to achieve this goal in our witness.

The Place of the Law in Evangelism: With the aid of the Holy Spirit (who is in the business of convicting of sin, righteousness and judgment—Jn. 16:8-11) we can use the sharp-edged scalpel of the law to expose the abscess of sin in the nature of unbelievers.[7] As noted previously, most people aren't hostile to Christianity; they're just indifferent. Psychology and sociology have told people their guilt is not real; they just haven't adjusted to their environment or social situation yet. They are not responsible for many of their actions. Such "modern" people do not measure themselves by God's absolutes but by comparison with others— what is normal in society. So their conscience is quieted, and they become unconcerned.

What will show people like this their spiritual poverty? They need to be lovingly shocked. They will never submit to radical heart surgery if they do not see their true guilt before a holy God. Their security is false. They think there is peace when there isn't. No wonder indifferent sinners look askance when told, "You need Christ as your Savior!" You can read their minds even if they do not say it: "Me? Need a Savior? That's for people who are lost!" They think their house is in order. Not perfect, but not badly out of line either. They have never used the level of God's law to check the angles of their total being. Our job is to bring that true level alongside their emotions, thoughts, actions, words, desires. Some passages of Scripture are ideal for reading with a non-Christian. Here are four that are scalpel sharp:

1. The Ten Commandments (Ex. 20)—Ask non-Christians to take a test. Go quickly through the commandments; ask how many they have broken. Many people think they have done fairly well on half or more—and the ones they have failed to keep were those that all of us slip up on now and then. Then go back over the commandments one by one and show the extent of them. Most people then see they have broken every one. If they remain unconvinced, mention James 2:10—breaking even one law brings condemnation from a wholly righteous God.

2. The Sermon on the Mount (Mt. 5—7)—This address describes the Christian's inner life (beatitudes) and actions. You may use this to explain the full implications of the Ten Commandments. For the climax you can show that unless a person's righteousness exceeds the righteousness of the scribes and Pharisees that person shall never enter the kingdom of heaven (Mt. 5:20). You can detail the scrupulous life of these Jewish religious people and ask, "Have you done better?" You can then explain the difference between external righteousness and heart righteousness.[8]

3. The Moral Young Man (Lk. 18:18-30)—Here is a moral person. Jesus explains that in breaking one commandment (coveting, the tenth commandment), the young man is not right with God. His heart is far from loving God. He is guilty. We can see why the disciples ask, "Who then can be saved?" (If anybody would have made it, this fellow should have.) Christ points out that it is impossible for man to save himself; however, with God all things are possible.

4. Paul's Life (Phil. 3:4-11; Rom. 7:7-13)—Paul was another person who seemed to have everything in a religious sense. He was a very moral and zealous individual. What made him give up all of his credentials? What led him to make the statement that those things that formed the basis of his security were no longer of any importance? Why did he desire to be identified with Christ? He had had a formal adherence to God's law. Now he saw this was not sufficient. He needed the righteousness of another—a perfect representative—with whom he could identify by faith.

What brought this proud man low? It was God's law; again, it was the last commandment. Coveting is something we do with our hearts, not our hands or feet. Suddenly, Paul saw the deep spirituality of the law, and it "killed" him. It revealed his sinfulness to him, put a sentence of death over any of his self-righteous efforts, leaving mercy as the only remedy that could save him.

In *Pilgrim's Progress* John Bunyan has illustrated that it is the function of the law to reveal our sin. Initially, Pilgrim (Graceless) finds out the strength of the law when he wanders out of the narrow way to the Celestial City. He is duped by Mr. Worldly Wiseman who points him to a broad and easy way which "will get you to the same destination." So he heads toward the town of Morality where he is to get help from Mr. Legality. Soon the road becomes exceedingly steep, and he finds himself climbing a mountain. The rocks hang over the road and threaten to crush him. Smoke and fire come out of the hill. With each step the pack on his back (a symbol of sin) gets heavier. Evangelist brings Pilgrim back in the way and rebukes him for trying to climb Mt. Sinai (the place where the law was given in the Old Testament).

Later, Pilgrim, now called Christian, is shown the meaning of certain principles in Scripture by one called Interpreter. Let John Bunyan tell this in his own words:

Then he took him by the hand, and led him into a very large parlour that was full of dust, because never swept; the which, after he had reviewed a little while, the INTERPRETER called for a man to sweep. Now, when he began to sweep, the dust began so abundantly to fly about, that CHRISTIAN had almost therewith been choked. Then said the INTERPRETER to a damsel that stood by, "Bring hither the water, and sprinkle the room;" the which, when she had done, it was swept and cleansed with pleasure.

Then said CHRISTIAN, "What means this?"

The INTERPRETER answered, "This parlour is the heart of a man that was never sanctified by the sweet grace of the gospel: the dust is his original sin and inward corruptions, that have defiled the whole man. He that began to sweep at first is the law; but she that brought water, and did sprinkle it, is the gospel. Now, whereas thou sawest that, so soon as the first began to sweep, the dust did so fly about, that the room by him could not be cleansed, but that thou wast almost choked therewith: this is to show thee that the law, instead of cleansing the heart, by its working, from sin, doth revive, put strength into, and increase it in the soul, even as it doth discover and forbid it; for it doth not give power to subdue (Rom. 5:20; 7:9; 1 Cor. 15:56).

"Again, as thou sawest the damsel sprinkle the room with water, upon which it was cleansed with pleasure (ease)—this is to show thee that when the gospel comes, in the sweet and precious influences thereof, to the heart, then I say, even as thou sawest the damsel lay the dust by sprinkling the floor with water, so is sin vanquished and subdued; and the soul made clean through the faith of it, and consequently fit for the King of Glory to inhabit."[9]

Calvin explains, the law is a preparation for the gospel. Its function is to call the conscience into judgment and wound it with fear. Scripture describes the law as a schoolmaster (an old-fashioned pedagogue with stern words and a whip) who leads us to Christ (Gal. 3:24). The teaching of God's standard is needed today. To use this schoolmaster would do much to humble nonbelievers and remove superficiality from man-centered evangelism.

The law sends us to the gospel so that we may be justified. The gospel sends us to the law to find out what our duty is now that we are justified. The place of God's moral law in the life of a Christian has also been neglected.[10]

The Place of Love in Evangelism: The law *convicts,* but it is powerless to *turn* a person. Such a turning occurs as unbelievers are wooed by God's love, for instance as they hear the story of Christ's life and death. The Holy Spirit in regeneration instills in the hearts of unbelievers a change of mind about their former life (repentance) and an irresistible drawing toward the One who shows mercy (faith). Conversion is then both a turning from *and* a turning toward. Paul knew that the Thessalonians were elect because of the effect the gospel had in their lives. They had turned to God from idols (1 Thess. 1:4-10).

It is necessary for an unbeliever not only to be convicted of sin but to apprehend the *grace* of God, thus laying hold of Christ crucified and risen. If we only show sin as exposing people to God's justice, then God will be a monster from whom a person will run. God, outside of Christ, will be terrifying to unbelievers who have enlightened consciences. Therefore, the doctrine of repentance is always to be presented in conjunction with grace. "Repentance and forgiveness of sins will be preached in his name . . ." (Lk. 24: 47). This last phrase does not just mean "in his authority," but in the Old Testament sense of "name" it denotes the full mercy and character of God. In Acts 26:20 we see Paul summarizing his ministry as a preaching of repentance and turning to God. But what encourages a person to turn to him? Three verses later we see Paul holding up a crucified Savior and promising life. Yes, we need to face unbelievers with the law as seen in judgment passages in Scripture, but it is the dying Savior on a *cross* who causes us to hate sin and surrender to love.

First, the cross shows us how heinous sin is. Why was Christ hung there? To give his life as a ransom for lost sheep. What was happening to him while there? He was taking upon himself all the punishment that should have been meted out to sinners. He was being made sin. So, the meaning of the cross is to be found not in the physical suffering, the scorning, the forsaking by the disciples. No. In the crucifixion the vertical, not the horizontal dimension, is central. God did not spare his own Son, but freely delivered him up so that we might go free. Every other manifestation of divine judgment against sin has always been deserved. At Calvary, the innocent Son was punished. Here we see the exceeding sinfulness of sin.

Second, the cross reveals a way of forgiveness consistent with the justice of God. How can God be just and do anything other than condemn the sinner? He provided a way out by having the judge stand in the place of the condemned.

Third, the cross demonstrates the love of God. God so loved that he *gave*. God's attributes of mercy and his disposition to pardon are made clear. How can one look upon his sins in the face of Calvary and not be moved?[11]

Dr. C. John Miller is fond of reminding would-be evangelists that we should be careful of separating repentance from the love of God. If we do, we will only lead people to *penance*. Rather, we need to present the law of God within the context of the love of God. Yes, we have sinned against law, but we have also sinned against *grace!* Even so, God still loves. He has free grace for sinners. No one should think of grace as locked in a box. Like the converted slave trader turned hymn writer, John Newton, we proclaim grace as costly but free. If you are thirsty, you can come and buy it. But you will not need money, as the price has already been paid by another. Without money, come to Jesus Christ and buy! (Is. 55:1-8).

In our witnessing let us do all we can to picture Christ as standing, arms outstretched, offering grace to sinners. They have sinned against God's goodness (which was designed to lead them to repentance). They have sinned against Christ himself, not just an abstract ethical standard. As Dr. Miller says, grace is available to repentant sinners. It will cover even the sin of despising the cross.

Let us open up the love of God to sinners in a striking and winsome way. How? By holding up Christ before the eyes of unbelievers. Then they can look to Jesus just as Israel in the wilderness looked on the bronze serpent (Jn. 3:14-15). As the Jews forsook all other remedies, faith poured itself in through their open eyes! Can we say with Paul that before the eyes of unbelievers we have clearly portrayed Christ as crucified (Gal. 3:1)? There is a need for more preaching from the Gospels in our day. We should be using episodes from the Gospels in our personal witnessing as well. The loving encounters Christ had with the poor, sick, blind, leprous, tax collector, religious hypocrite and prostitute need to be vividly recreated in the minds of sinners. They need to identify themselves with these people. The sheer power of these simple incidents can reveal the inmost thoughts of many unbelievers and can show Jesus to be the intriguing, attractive and overwhelming Savior that he is. Over and over again we must focus on the stunning and extensive love of Jesus. There is too much moralizing in evangelical preaching and not enough magnifying of grace in Jesus. Many sections of Scripture shock us with God's love. Here are some passages that melt hard hearts:

1. The Woman at the Well (Jn. 4)—See how tenderly Christ puts his finger on her sin. He speaks the truth in love. How apt is his use of water as a thirst quencher for a dissatisfied lover. He knows her whole life, but he offers her himself. Compare the story of Hosea choosing a promiscuous woman for his wife.

2. The Blind Man (Jn. 9)—Jesus heals this man and lets him see again. But he doesn't see too clearly for a while. He has limited understanding of the person who healed him. He is doubted by friends, forsaken by parents and ridiculed by the ministers. Jesus goes and finds him, completing his understanding and fortifying his faith. Yet all this display of God's love is consistent with this man's God-ordained blindness. For the really unfortunate people are those who claim they can see but are really blind, and therefore their guilt remains. His blindness was to display God's glory, and it worked out for his good. Since he was blind he could see his need of Jesus more clearly!

3. The Lost and the Found (Lk. 15)—The three stories in this one chapter all have the same point. Jesus had been criticized by the religious people for spending time with the needy. He shows in the incidents of the lost sheep, the lost coin and the lost son that it is his purpose to seek that which is lost. When one is found there is joy in heaven. God loves sinners. They are precious to him. He rejoices in them. His banner over them is love.

4. The Woman Forgiven Much (Lk. 7:36-50)—A woman who lived a very sinful life came to Jesus while he was eating dinner at the home of a religious leader. She washed Jesus' dusty feet with expensive perfume and tears. Then she dried them with her hair.

The religious people objected to Jesus having such a woman touch him. He replies that God loves to be generous, canceling even the largest of debts. She was passing on the magnanimous love shown to her in forgiveness of her numerous sins.

One of the oldest and wisest of the Protestant creedal statements is the Westminster Confession. In it we read this definition of repentance (italics are mine):

> By it [repentance] a sinner, out of the sight and sense, not only of the danger, but also of the filthiness and odiousness of his sins, as contrary to the holy nature and righteous *law of God, and* upon the apprehension of His *mercy in Christ* to such as are penitent, so grieves for, and hates his sins, as to turn from them all unto God, purposing and endeavoring to walk with Him in all the ways of His commandments.

Today's surgeons of the heart are not using their best knife! No wonder the conviction of sin and repentance, signifying the recovery of the patient, are often lacking. The Holy Spirit uses the law to convict. For an example of the heart language of a convicted sinner, study Psalm 51. Both law and love are basic ingredients in God's powerful gospel.

Compare our sinfulness with a diseased tree. What do you do when you find deformed and diseased fruit on a tree? Can the problem be solved by simply picking off the bad fruit? Of course not. You have to get to the root of the problem; you must change the very life of the tree that is found in the sap. So also with our sinful natures. We cannot be changed by altering a few of our bad habits. Reformation will not do, for the disease of sin has captured our very life system. We need regeneration—a new heart.

To begin to get an idea of our guilt, think of recording every action and thought for the last twenty-four hours in a diary. If you lost that diary, how would you feel? God knows our inmost thoughts, and one day we shall stand before him and nothing shall be hid (Mt. 10:26; 1 Cor. 4:5). After the dark clouds of the bad news, the good news shines in a rainbow of bright colors. Paul announces his theme as the gospel in Romans 1:16-17, yet immediately portrays nothing but bad news all the way until Romans 3: 21! Unbelievers must see themselves as guilty rebels under judgment and unable to save themselves.

III.   Christ—the Merciful Redeemer

Once we have helped people see the true nature of their sickness, there is only one cure. Other religions do not have this radical view of sinfulness; therefore, the salvation they offer is also not as radical. Those who have difficulty understanding why Christ is the only way to God and want to argue the unjustness of this (the all-roads-lead-to-heaven theory) have probably not seen the real character of man (a creature with a sinful nature) nor the true character of God (the Creator who is holy and loving). Much of witnessing is bringing people to understand and feel the extent of their helplessness and corruption. Since most come to us with sparse God-consciousness and little sense of their sinfulness, we must spend time going back over the first two points of the outline.

Francis Schaeffer was once asked the question, "What would you do if you met a really modern man on a train and you had just an hour to talk to him about the gospel?" He replied, "I've said over and over, I would spend 45-50 minutes on the negative, to really show him his dilemma—that he is morally dead—then I'd take 10-15 minutes to preach the Gospel. I believe that much of our evangelistic and personal work today is not clear simply because we are too anxious to get to the answer without having a man realize the real cause of his sickness, which is true moral guilt (and not just psychological guilt feelings) in the presence of God."[12] You will find as people begin to grasp the significance of God as Creator and man as the sinful creature, you can explain in a most direct and powerful way who Christ is.

Yet, here again man-centered evangelism is often deficient. It tends to focus on one of Christ's roles (offices) to the exclusion of others. It may be well versed in presenting Christ as priest who, via a substitutionary sacrifice of himself for sin, effected a reconciliation between the sinner and God. Yet, unhappily, it often misses the importance of his life of perfectly fulfilling the law (active obedience) and thereby gaining for those whom he represents a perfect righteousness. In the death of Christ (passive obedience), the broken law's penalty is borne for us. Yet Christ has not just put us back in the garden (a state of innocence or of moral neutrality) but has put a robe of righteousness on us. A simple pencil can be used to illustrate this. The eraser is the blood of Christ cleansing us from all sin (1 Jn. 1:7). The lead is the righteous life of Christ by which he fulfilled all the commands of God required of us. Not only are all our sins erased, but a mark of righteousness is written next to our names (Rom. 8:3-4). He is sin-bearer and purity-bestower.

In my gospel outline I've used two other terms to summarize Christ's functions. He is a master (king) and a teacher (prophet). Let us look at his kingly role first. Can you have only the Savior (sin-bearer) Christ in your heart? No, it is impossible to divide Christ. If he truly comes into your life, *all* of him enters. The overwhelming usage of the word *Lord* in the book of Acts shows us clearly how Christ was presented to nonbelievers. The phrase "accept Christ as your personal Savior" is not found. Rather, "God has made . . . Jesus . . . both Lord and Christ" (Acts 2:36); "Who are you, Lord?" (Acts 9:5); "Believe in the Lord Jesus" (Acts 16:31).

These apostles were not preaching salvation by "making Christ Lord of your life" in a good-works fashion. He is already Lord; and therefore, our evangelistic call must be to come to him as to the feet of a monarch, in submission to his person and authority. We cannot come to a king with one hand behind our backs, standing upright, signifying secret reservations and unwillingness to give over control of our lives. We are not in a position to bargain. We must bow—with both hands outstretched and open.

This is the picture of the true penitent's attitude of heart (not that we are able to render perfect obedience). Because we are not whole people we cannot give a holistic response. Yet God receives the part for the whole, the seed as evidence the flower will bloom.

In the mercy of God, it is later in our Christian lives that we are shown the implications of our initial submission to him as king.

I cannot point to the specific day on which I crossed over the line to be on the Lord's side. I can remember well that period in my life during my sophomore and junior years in high school when I first began to have an attitude of love to Christ and surrender to his will. I used to live for the weekends, but by Sunday night I would return to the loneliness of my bedroom and express my deep dissatisfaction, telling him to take over. I knew very little of the theology of Christ's lordship, but I still embraced it. I wanted someone to rule my unruly heart.

I realize now how gracious Christ was to not overwhelm me at that point with the specific forms his mastery over me would take. I did not comprehend that his lordship would include my custom-built car, date life, money, vocation. Nevertheless, I handed him the notebook of my life and sincerely asked him to write in it what he wanted. All new Christians are born spiritual babes; we don't expect them to be full-fledged disciples immediately. Yet there is an instinctive attitude of wanting to embrace Christ's lordship in every truly converted person. Christ will exercise his sovereignty by daily bringing us to a willing bondage under an easy yoke and light burden in which his commands are not grievous. What a tremendous liberation!

As our teacher-prophet, he is the one who supremely reveals God himself and his will. When we make this clear in evangelism we set the stage for a person to know where he must go from now on for guidance and who is the only one who has the words of eternal life. In his special commission to his disciples, Jesus appointed his disciples to give the written, inspired interpretation of his revelation in history. Christ as our prophet will do this through the Holy Spirit by bringing "all things to their remembrance," so that the believer will have a "more sure word of prophecy"—the Bible (Jn. 14:26; 2 Pet. 1:19-21). We are *not* to look to seers, mystics, mediums or even our own hunches, supposed prophecies, or personal revelations for determining God's will.

Jesus is alive today. We find this truth gripped and fired the early evangelists in Acts. He really rose from the dead; if he did not, then we are wasting our time. Picture a ship in a raging storm being broken up on cruel rocks just offshore. The people of the town man a small boat and struggle against seemingly insurmountable odds to rescue the ship's crew. In anguish the people on the shore wait and watch for the first sign of the return of the rescue boat. At last it appears through the wind-whipped sea. Too anxious to wait any longer someone yells out from shore at the top of his lungs, "Any survivors?" Each second seems an age, and then the brief and crushing reply comes, "No, all are lost." The group on shore, bewildered, does not know what to do or say. Finally, one man cries out with the little that is in him, "Three cheers for the attempt," and the crowd does its best to raise its voice in compliance.

And what of the resurrection of Jesus? If he did not really conquer death, then the best that can be said is, "Three cheers for the attempt."

We wish people to see Jesus as the God-man who is the only way to life. A prairie fire was whipped along by the wind so fast that it overtook all creatures in its path. One family, seeing the impossibility of outrunning the blaze, began a back fire and then covered themselves with earth as they lay in the midst of the already burned-out circle. The roaring fire met the back fire and it burned only up to the edge of that burned-over area; then went right around it, continuing its hungry race. That family was saved. They knew the only safe place was where the fire had already burned.

The fire of God's wrath has touched down at one particular point in history. And when it did, it utterly consumed a man as he hung on a cross. It did not burn a large area, but it finalized God's work of judgment. The fire of God's wrath will come again in history. This time it will consume the whole earth. Will there be any place to hide? Only on the hill where that cross stood, there where the fire has already burned. A person is forgiven if he identifies with Christ who on the cross bore God's judgment for sin. Jesus

Christ is our burned-over area; the only safe hiding place.

In presenting the whole gospel, we must vividly present the whole Christ—in all his roles.

IV. Our Necessary Response

An inherent part of the biblical gospel is the call to respond. No evangelist is worthy of our support, no matter how superb his presentation of truth about God, man and Christ, if he then walks away without lovingly urging people to respond.

On the other hand, method-centered evangelism is too active. Considering how important it is not to "let the fish get away," whole manuals have been written for "successful" fishing. Often sinners are confused rather than helped at this point. A physical action (signing a card, repeating a prayer, walking forward, raising a hand, standing up and so on) are made the sign of an inner spiritual reality. The man-centered evangelist turns into a salesman, creating undue psychological pressure. It is here we most graphically betray our weak theology. If God is sovereign and if the person's conviction is of the Holy Spirit, then God can finish what he has begun. Our mistrust of the Spirit's power is serious at this point.

Instead of these tactics, offer passages like Isaiah 53:1-11, Psalm 51:1-17 and Galatians 2:20, and then in most cases leave them alone. God will finish what he has begun. We can urge them to pray and seek for mercy and to keep on doing so until God answers. We need to direct seeking sinners to come and rejoice with us when they know God has answered (inner witness, Rom. 8: 14-16) and they see their motives and actions begin to change (outer evidence, 1 Jn.). Then we can complement the work of the Holy Spirit by helping them to become grounded in Scripture and involved in fellowship.

We must not usurp the work of the Spirit whose task is to bring to repentance and faith, and then to seal new believers. Too often *we* have tried to give assurance of salvation by listening to their prayers, seeing their tears, and thus judging them sincere. We then instruct them to put their name in John 3:16 and never doubt God again. ("For God so loved _____.") But the Spirit witnesses to our life assurance policy not some counselor. No wonder the church is full of professors but few possessors!

The Bible teaches that when people respond to the gospel, they both *can* and *should* have assurance of their salvation. This was John's purpose in writing his first letter. "I write these things to you who believe in the name of the Son of God so that you may know that you have eternal life" (1 Jn. 5:13). There are those who consider themselves saved who need to discover they are lost. There are those who still consider themselves lost who are truly saved. How can this be? Let me describe two types of people.

The first type has assurance that is based on self-deception. They believe God has saved them but continue to live a deliberately sinful life. This is presumption not assurance. They presume on God's grace rather than being assured of it. They are still lost and they need to examine their basis for assurance.

A second type vacillates in the certainty of their own salvation. They do not doubt that God can save, but doubt rather that God has saved *them*. They can have many reasons for this vacillation, and they may or may not still be unbelievers. Since assurance of one's salvation is not automatic on becoming a Christian, one may be a true believer, yet lack assurance that one is. True believers can be confused about their salvation because of unresolved doubt, failure to deal with known sin in their lives, temptation, physical and emotional fatigue, an overly sensitive conscience, wrong teaching, or God himself sending a trial and withdrawing from them.[13] So the confused, along with the presumptuous and the uncertain, need a clear understanding of the doctrine of assurance.[14]

The question is, "How do I know that I am a Christian?" This is a different question from, "How do I become a Christian?" and therefore has a completely different answer. Yet too often people respond to these questions in the same way, and those who seek help in their quest for assurance do not find it. The answer to the second question is, "You become a Christian through repentance toward God and faith in Christ alone as Savior and Lord." The answer to the first question is, "You know that you have become a Christian (that God has answered prayer and regenerated you) by a threefold result in your life."

The first pillar of assurance is a trust in the promises of God as being promises to you. You count them true and take them personally. The second is the beginning of a change in your attitudes and actions corresponding to the fruit of the Spirit (Gal. 5) and the marks of salvation (1 Jn.). The third is the inner witness of God's Spirit to your spirit that you are his child (Rom. 8). These three pillars are like giant candles whose light reveals our regenerated nature. Scripture tells us to "examine yourselves to see whether you are in the faith; test yourselves" (2 Cor. 13:5). This is not morbid introspection. In biblical self-examination we look to what God says should be true of a believer and see if it is true of our lives during the past week or month. We must not consider only the last hour or day, but also a longer time period, for we find winters when no fruit is evident, even in the souls of true Christians.

We must not, however, condone persistent and prolonged disobedience to the known will of God on the part of professing Christians. God's purpose is to smash such "assurance," for it is mere presumption. This is the point of all the warnings and "ifs" in the letter to the Hebrews. Professing Christians shall not escape *if* they neglect God's great salvation. If such people are merely labeled "carnal Christians," they are led into a dangerous false security. Using the term *carnal* as an adjective to modify the word *Christian* leads to the misconception that a person can be both of the world (continuing in a life characterized by fleshly attitudes and actions) and of Christ. The Bible nowhere allows this. It speaks of Christians who have *areas* of carnality in their lives (jealousy, quarreling, personal loyalties, 1 Cor. 3:1-4), but never of Christians whose whole lives over a prolonged period are saturated with disobedience. How can Christ be in a life but not on the throne of that life? Where else in our hearts could Christ the king reside if not ruling from the throne of our lives?

What does the first type of person lacking assurance need to be told, those professing believers whose lives are characterized by sin? It would be confusing to urge "more of the Spirit" upon them when they may yet be unconverted! The kindest thing we can do is to turn them to the Scriptures so they can evaluate their *present* lives not past deeds or experiences. Here they will find objective descriptions of the attitudes and actions of true believers. They are not to measure themselves by their own (or others') traditions and subjective standards of true spirituality, for this would lead them into a quagmire of uncertainty. Educating their consciences with God's doctrine about the three marks of saving faith will free them from enslavement to their darkened consciences, the expectations of others, and the use of feelings as the criterion for and content of faith.

Is it kind to shatter a person's hope of salvation? Yes, because without scriptural grounds, it is nothing more than a false hope. A hope of acceptance by God based on such things as going forward in a meeting, praying a suggested prayer, imitating the experience of others, joining a church, attending many Christian meetings, studying the Bible regularly, helping others, feeling good in a religious service, or having a strong conviction that he is right with God is a hope not founded on biblical truths. Perhaps a person may trust in the doctrine of election or in theological precision or in baptism. He or she may have a sentimental belief in the general providence of God: "God has been good to me; God will take care of me." Yet one can be involved in any or all of these activities without *ever* looking to Jesus Christ as the only Savior and Lord. Without this there is no salvation. Without this there is no assurance. Let us in kindness alert that person to what Christ will say to some on the day of judgment. "Not everyone who says to me, 'Lord, Lord,' will enter the kingdom of heaven, but only he who does the will of my Father who is in heaven. Many will say to me on that day, 'Lord, Lord, did we not prophesy in your name, and in your name drive out demons and perform many miracles?' Then I will tell them plainly, 'I never knew you. Away from me, you evildoers!' " (Mt. 7:21-23).

Suppose we are dealing with the second type of person lacking assurance, true believers who are really tormented and need to know of their security in Christ. Again, the kind thing is to bring the sure Word of God, with its infallible promises, alongside the grace they find exists in their changed hearts. The Spirit will then enable believers to say with assurance, "I am a child of God and will be forever." This great comfort and encouragement does not come through a private revelation of the Spirit (a witness of the Spirit apart from or in addition to the Bible). Assurance is effected not by imparting new revelation to a person's heart, but by applying what is already revealed in Scripture, namely, the truth that believers shall be saved.[15]

When we sin it is to be expected that our assurance of salvation will be weakened. God is keeping us from complacency and warning us not to play with sin. God, in mercy, will not allow children of his to be comfortable in sin. He makes us restless, even to the point of questioning our salvation, so that we may not presume on his favor but, instead, relish his grace. Often we recognize our salvation not by victory over sin but by the warfare that is still going on within us. Comfort and encouragement do not come from outward circumstances of "success" but rather from a drawing near to God with a true heart in full assurance of faith. It is knowing that nothing can separate us from the love of God in Christ Jesus our Lord. Boldness coupled with humility is the result. Our assurance must be founded, built up and established on the mercy of God alone. It can be further established when we review ourselves before God and find evidence of his dwelling and reigning within us in the deeds God has enabled us to do.[16] Our eternal security does not depend on any past actions but on our present attitude toward Christ. Just as earthly parents can expect physical growth in their children, so we can expect to see a gradual change in the lives of God's children.

Let me conclude by specifically mentioning some guidelines. Since we cannot read other people's hearts and discern their true standing (saved or lost) before God, let us not try to take over the work of the Holy Spirit. Rather, we should help them to measure themselves by God's standard. We refrain from minimizing sin, we portray grace as truly free, and we remind them of the three tenses of salvation: I have been saved (Eph. 2:8), I am being saved (1 Cor. 1:18), I will be saved (Rom. 5:9). The basis for assurance of salvation is threefold: the promises of God made real to the heart, the inner testimony of God's Spirit to our spirit, and the production of attitudes and actions congruent with the fruit of the Spirit and God's commandments. This last objective pillar is delineated in John's first letter. It is helpful to suggest that a person who has made a profession of faith read this epistle keeping the following points in mind.

1. Test of consciousness of sin. 1 John 1:8, 10.
2. Test of obedience. 1 John 2:3-5, 29.
3. Test of freedom from habitual sin. 1 John 3:9; 5:18.
4. Test of love for other Christians. 1 John 3:14; 4:7-8.
5. Test of belief. 1 John 5:1.
6. Test of overcoming the world and Satan. 1 John 2:13-14; 5:4.

The command to "turn to God in repentance and have faith in our Lord Jesus" summarizes the gospel invitation (Acts 20:21). It is important to have both these elements urged upon non-Christians who are under conviction.[17] The lack of emphasis on repentance as an aspect of easy-believism is regrettable. Although turning and trusting may be presented separately at times in the Bible, as we compare Scripture with Scripture, we see that they are two sides of one coin. We must avoid pressing one on unbelievers without the other. Repentance without faith will lead to sorrow and mere legalistic resolutions (2 Cor. 7:10; compare Cain, Saul and Judas). Faith without repentance is unfounded optimism leading to self-deception. As Packer so aptly puts it, "mere creedence without trusting and mere remorse without turning, do not save."[18]

Again we see the importance of defining our words and not speaking in general terminology without specific application to the life of non-Christians. (See appendix B, worksheet 1.)

Wrapping up this brief commentary on a few distinctives of a God-centered gospel, I conclude with the importance of defining faith. Saving faith has as its object the person of Christ, the Atoner, not just certain facts about the atonement. The latter view makes faith equivalent to mental assent. And the church is filled with people who add one more fact to their minds. Yes, there are other aspects of the work of Christ (Incarnation, obedient life, resurrection, ascension), but these are not the objects of saving faith either. The whole person is to respond to the whole Christ. The essence of real faith is trust—akin to drinking, eating, submitting, identifying with a person. Such faith does not receive a divided Christ but a whole Christ. There is not one exhortation in Scripture to *Christians* to "accept Christ as Lord." Rather, they are to work out the implications of their *initial* relationship to him. Christians are urged to daily surrender after their initial and most basic surrender that took place at their regeneration (Rom. 6:17-18, 22; 12:1-2; Col. 2:6). Saving faith is not a look backward to the cross in the past but a look forward to Christ in the present. It is the implanting of an attitude.

As we discuss the call for both repentance and faith in our gospel proclamation, I want to make a special plea for teaching the magnificent doctrine of justification by faith. Picture a courtroom scene. God has on his robes of justice and we are standing before him. We would expect to hear the word *guilty* as the gavel of God's judgment comes down with a thud. But what do we hear? "Acquitted." Yes! Justification is God saying, "Go free," to undeserving sinners. We are not condemned because his anger against our sin has been fully satisfied by the free donation of an alien righteousness on our behalf.

It is astounding how little evangelicals really understand this; consequently, they have a wrong emphasis in both evangelism and in the Christian life. The truths of justification give the founda-

tion for Christian witness. Robert Horn says, "Justification holds all
the aspects of the Gospel in focus. Indeed it *is* the Gospel: without it we have no good news to tell; leave out justification and we
leave out a great deal more than just a word . . . without justification, everything becomes superficial. . . . The point is that justification represents a whole perspective."[19] As we respond with the
gratitude inevitably kindled by free grace, our turning and trusting
pleases God.

Truth: The Yardstick of Evangelism

We should be concerned because the gospel message is being
blunted in our day and one *effect* is scorched earth in many youth-
ful hearts. I meet those who say, "I tried Christianity; it didn't
work." Or, far worse, "I know I'm a Christian; here's the card I
signed five years ago. Besides, the counselor told me never to
doubt God." We sadly notice the dust-laden Bible on the shelf. No
one, not even the most consistently God-centered evangelist, can
avoid dropouts and deformed babies. On the other hand, I do not
say the gospel is wholly lost or that God may not often work
through a defective evangelistic presentation. He is a sovereign
God. No one can claim to have the perfect gospel outline or the
right approach for each situation. We all are humbled by the
sovereign and compassionate God who works as he wills to bring
someone to himself. The *amount* of truth God will use to regen-
erate a person is something we cannot dictate. God, in the wind of
the Spirit, blows where he wills. Yet, it is *truth* God always uses;
it is never our *tool* (pamphlet, outline, program or famous speaker)
in evangelism that works. All success is God's. To him alone be the
glory.

The sovereignty of God never excuses *us* from responsibility.
If we are not concerned to present a whole gospel, then we are unconcerned to glorify God in all that we do. Are we content to follow the pattern of programmed witnessing dictated by man-centered evangelists (albeit well-meaning) who have abbreviated the
message and unconsciously adopted techniques inappropriate to

convey the gospel of God's grace? Are we willing to evaluate humbly our personal witness and all else that we use that professes to be "evangelistic" by this yardstick: what *truth* was *taught?*

In this attempt to evaluate the character of contemporary evangelism, it has been necessary to speak forcefully and by way of contrast so that I could communicate what disturbs me in the new gospel reduction. Differences among Christians must be understood and honestly faced. Under the cloak of Christian unity, a cease-fire has been declared on doctrinal discussion regarding evangelism. Doctrine becomes a word with a bad connotation for it is labeled as the source of division among Christians. I am not interested in theological nit-picking over minor teachings in Scripture. What I am saying is that major gospel truths are being ignored. In the interest of unity, "some evangelicals are jettisoning any serious attempt to exhibit truth and antithesis. This often finishes up by denying, in practice if not in theory, the importance of doctrinal truth as such. Cooperation and unity that do not lead to purity of life and purity of doctrine are just as faulty and incomplete as an orthodoxy which does not lead to a concern for, and reaching out towards, those who are lost."[20] I believe it is ignorance of an overall systematic theological frame of reference that will bring about divisions among us as each person exalts his pet doctrine. A balanced theology would unite us (Eph. 4:13-16). It is ignorance that often divides while doctrine can unite us.

None of us is so naive to think all differences among Christians would be solved in our day if we returned to a theological basis for evangelism. Nevertheless, it is still imperative to challenge each other to look into the Scriptures again and again in order to make us more self-conscious of the doctrines that shape our methods. Even if we must agree to disagree on certain points, we will know clearly what they are; our fellowship will be more honest, and our children can take up studying where we have left off. We must never give up praying that new light will break upon the church as she seriously studies the Bible.[21]

One place to start could be an agreement to alter the unbiblical practice of separating doctrine from experience, thus making doctrine secondary in importance to practice. The movement in the New Testament is *from* doctrine *to* experience. To reverse this order or to say it doesn't matter, leads to a contentless Christ trip. Doctrine and life have been married by God. It is not moral declension that leads to doctrinal declension, but the reverse. Romans 1 clearly shows that when men and women turn away from the truth, moral declension follows. So, let us not hush up any Priscilla or Aquilla who will take us aside to expound the way of God more accurately to us (Acts 18:26). Let us be willing to test our spiritual experiences and evangelistic practices by Scripture.

At times we may reach an impasse over doctrine and go our separate ways in evangelism. Does this mean we cut ourselves off completely from other true Christians? In such a case we must also manifest love by looking to specific activities we can share, because in some areas we do possess a unity of truth. Christians must display their calling to manifest the character of God's chief attributes of holiness/purity and love/humility in all their personal relationships.

In seeking the *recovery* of the gospel for our day, God forbid that we should ever *cover* it with complexity for the unbelievers. "No sincere Christian intends to deceive sinners. In love for souls, true evangelicals invariably present some profound truths in their witnessing. Yet by the unconscious omission of essential ingredients of the Gospel, many fail to communicate even that portion of God's Word which they mean to convey. When a half truth is presented as the whole truth, it becomes an untruth."[22] God help us to teach the *maximum* amount of truth about the glorious God who is Creator and Redeemer in a winsome, lucid, bold way to as many of this world's children as we can.

Note: *"The Greatest Test", an alternative to the gospel outline presented in this chapter, is available in a low-cost booklet. See pages 176-177 for more information.*

Part II

To the Whole Person: Conversion of the Total Person

*Brothers loved by God, we know that he has chosen you,
because our gospel came to you not simply with words, but also
with power, with the Holy Spirit and with deep conviction.
You know how we lived among you for your sake. You became
imitators of us and of the Lord; in spite of severe suffering,
you welcomed the message with the joy given by the Holy Spirit.
And so you became a model to all the believers in Macedonia
and Achaia. The Lord's message rang out from you not only in
Macedonia and Achaia—your faith in God has become
known everywhere. Therefore we do not need to say anything
about it, for they themselves report what kind of reception
you gave us. They tell how you turned to God from idols to serve
the living and true God, and to wait for his Son from heaven,
whom he raised from the dead—Jesus, who rescues us from
the coming wrath.*
1 Thessalonians 1:4-10

4

Professors but Not Possessors

I t is not a new teaching to say that a person can profess faith in Christ without actually possessing Christ. It is sad to realize that a false profession of faith is frequent in the church. Most of us know people who seemed to be drawn toward the gospel and yet didn't step over the line of faith. Can this be the explanation for the conflict between statistics that show a large number of professing born-again Christians and the continuing moral tailspin of our nation? What I wish to do in this section is set forth the biblical view of conversion, a conversion of the whole personality in all its faculties, and contrast it with types of partial conversions.

Our desire must be nothing less than to see the whole individual converted. We are looking to God for changed persons—not just a response from one segment of a personality. God's regenerative work is a thorough renewing that involves all the faculties of mind, emotions and will. Scriptural language calls this a "new creation," a "new birth." People are either saved or lost. To weaken this radical but scriptural cleavage of mankind by suggesting a third category for people is an attack on the biblical doctrine of regeneration. There is no such thing as being a half Christian—for instance, being a "Christian" but not a Spirit-baptized Christian; being a "Christian" but not accepting Christ as Lord; being a "Christian" but living a life continually characterized by carnality.

A Christian has the Holy Spirit, being baptized, indwelt, sealed and sanctified by him (Acts 2:38-39; Rom. 8:9, 11, 13-15; 1 Cor. 3:16; 12:12-13; Eph. 1:13). A Christian has acknowledged the lordship of Christ (Acts 22:10; Rom. 10:9-10; 1 Jn. 5:1-5). All Christians turn away from sin (Rom. 6:1-14; 1 Jn. 3:3-10). It is the low level of spirituality among us that has caused the term *Christian* to become so insipid that we propose various adjectives to restore its flavor. I have no argument with any movement to raise the norm of our spiritual life. I suggest, though, that the best way to raise it is to deepen our understanding of regeneration, not tack on new dimensions. If God has already given us the greatest present in the world, will he withhold the ribbon? Nevertheless, we find our joy in the gift not decorations (Rom. 8:32).

The Normal Christian Conversion

Regeneration and *conversion* are words to describe two different ways of viewing salvation. Regeneration is viewing salvation from God's side; it is an instantaneous impartation of new life to the soul. We may or may not be conscious of the exact moment this happened to us. Conversion, on the other hand, is viewing salvation from our perspective. It is a *process* of the entire work of God's grace from the first dawning of understanding and seeking to the final closing with Christ in new birth. For some, this is a period of years; for others merely an hour. We respond in time to God's action in eternity.[1]

Lack of understanding of the *normal* stages of conversion has led to confused counseling on the part of well-meaning evangelists. To dispel this confusion, a closer look at the phases is helpful. But be advised, the Spirit does not always work according to our timetable. God does not limit himself to a specific design. There is a pattern, however, even amidst the unique circumstances surrounding a conversion like Paul's.[2] It helps to realize people are not always regenerated the first time they begin to call on the name of the Lord. To confuse the *first* workings of response in the conversion process with the *final* is extremely dangerous for non-Christians can be deluded into thinking they are saved before they really are. Our forefathers made some helpful distinctions in these areas. They called an unbeliever, apparently untouched by any saving operations of God's Spirit, a "sleeping sinner." An "awakened" or "seeking sinner" was one who had begun to respond to God's prior working of his Spirit. The positive response would manifest itself in a conviction of sin and an active call on Christ for salvation, which would result in the sinner willfully exercising faith and repentance. Each of these stages emphasizes a different relationship with God. Today, however, the tendency is to rush a person into the kingdom at the slightest indication of an interest in spiritual things. Jesus was cautious at times (Nicodemus, the moral young man) and tested the spiritual conviction of his would-be disciples.

What a joy it is to meet people prepared by God's Spirit to receive the gospel! We pray that the convicting power of the Holy Spirit will come upon these seeking and awakened sinners. We don't require them to stand outside the kingdom for months, but say, in the words of a hymn,[3]

Come, ye needy, come, and welcome;
   God's free bounty glorify;
True belief and true repentance,
   Every grace that brings us nigh;
Without money, without money, without money,
   Come to Jesus Christ and buy.
   Come to Jesus Christ and buy.

   . . . Jesus ready stands to save you,

Full of pity joined with power:
He is able, He is able, He is able,
   He is willing; doubt no more.
   He is willing, doubt no more.

We are anxious, in a good sense, to see such people move beyond a general sensitivity to the gospel, and so we point them and urge them toward Christ, the door. What can we do when we find someone who seems to be coming under conviction? Sometimes these people get stuck at the brink of decision. Here are some principles in guiding them:[4]

First, counsel them in a way that focuses on action not talk. In other words, resist counseling at length without giving them imperatives to act upon.

Second, urge them to cast themselves on the mercy of the Lord. We are not to hear their confessions and become their priest—for this may be a way they relieve their guilt.

Third, use the Bible in an effort to impress them with God's counsel not your wisdom.

Finally, we must be genuine—our entire emotional concern is to represent the Lord and to help the seeker. Specifically we should:

1. Encourage them—God is bringing them to a crisis.

2. Warn the hesitant and stubborn—not that they *can't* be saved, but they are not choosing to be saved.

3. Emphasize the sin there is in relapse—greater judgment accrues from greater knowledge (Heb. 6:4-6; 2 Pet. 2:21).

4. Encourage them not to neglect Christian meetings—"faith comes from hearing" (Rom. 10:17).

5. Allow for *no* margin of complacency; if the search is interminable, it is likely their fault.

6. Point them to a personal Savior—not just to meaning in life, peace of heart or the like—because the root of our rebellion is personal sin against God (Jer. 29:13).

7. Stress urgent, earnest seeking (Deut. 4:29).

8. Ask if they really desire a changed nature, if they really *want* to be saved.

9. Ask if they will yield to the Lord. He commands us to believe (Acts 17:30; 1 Jn. 3:23).

10. Challenge them to admit what sin they are clinging to.

11. Show them how to pray—suggest Psalm 51.

12. Explain that their duty is to transfer their trust to Christ and believe—now!

A Partial Response to the Gospel

Is it possible for a person sincerely to *profess* faith in Christ but not *possess* the real thing? Yes, certainly. A friend told me how he awakened to the fact that something was amiss in the body of Christ. He had been striving to incite love and obedience among some church young people and had been invited to speak to these "Christians." The weekend retreat was fast approaching, but he had no peace about the message he should bring. He began to wonder why it was that the faith of these young people always needed "jacking up." He began to wonder if they had any real faith in the first place. He was afraid of being thought of as fanatical or supercritical, but he decided to begin by asking the group some basic questions.

The first night of the retreat arrived, and he opened up with two questions: "How many of you, if you died tonight, would know you'd go to heaven?" All raised their hands. "How many of you really want to do the will of God—allowing that you can't obey *perfectly*—but you truly *purpose* in your heart to do it?" Only one-fifth raised their hands. How could he square the responses to these questions with clear biblical teaching that says that true salvation not only secures the forgiveness of rebels but their obedience as well (Heb. 5:9)? He decided to preach evangelistically that entire conference and saw many come to faith in Christ.

At a women's college I was having lunch in the dining hall with a student who had regularly attended the Inter-Varsity Christian Fellowship Bible studies. She seemed to have high morals and was kind to others. She had very little to say when it came to how the Scriptures were part of her life; she also failed to express any specific biblical content in her witness to non-Christians. She was friendly and outgoing. Many assumed that she was a Christian. I asked her to what she attributed her confidence that she was converted.

"When I was in ninth grade," she replied, "I remained in my church sanctuary after the morning service. It was a lovely day, and the sun was shining through the stained-glass windows creating vivid patterns. I felt all warm, good and peaceful."

I sat there waiting for her to say more, but that was it! Many people have a good hope but with absolutely no foundation for it.

Another girl at a state university came to me full of frustration. For a year she had been quite active in various Inter-Varsity activities. She prayed, read the Bible and sang heartily. Her peers assumed she was a Christian, but these were her words: "I need the friendship and acceptance of others. This school is so big. It's a lonely place. I didn't fit in with the wilder girls. The Christian group is so friendly. I fit in easily, but I can't face it any longer. I'm not really one of you. I've come to see I'm not a Christian."

Without a thorough understanding of the holistic approach to evangelism, such people who have never been converted will either continue being deceived about their true state and thus become a hindrance to the church, or they will drop out, joining the ranks of the disillusioned and either become numb or hostile to religion. Hardened by years of no response to the Word of God, relatively few of these people seem to get converted. We must help them and not mislead them.

God's Word is not silent on this issue either.

1. Parable of the Four Soils (Mt. 13:1-23)—Two of the seeds sown by the Sower begin to grow but do not mature, because the soil is bad. There is an initial response of joy, hearing, growth, but that response does not continue because of a lack of roots and shade. The thorns showed that the soil of the heart was not good.

2. Simon the Sorcerer (Acts 8:9-24)—This man is described as believing and desiring more spiritual power in his life. He was also baptized. Yet he is not truly converted for he offers money for spiri-

tual power (simony). Peter says he should perish and that Simon has "no part or share in this ministry, because your heart is not right before God. . . . You are full of bitterness and captive to sin."

3. Herod (Mt. 2:1-18)—Because we are so familiar with the outcome of Herod's inquiry for Christ, we forget that he impressed many with his "Christian" zeal at the first. He took an interest in the Bible; he sought out wise men to help him with prophecy; he went to the trouble of finding Christ. He did not ask Christ to be brought to him but, in apparent humility, wanted to go to him. Not only that, but he professed a correct view of Christ, for he said he wanted to worship him.

4. The Passover Crowd (Jn. 2:23-25)—Here are personal witnesses of Jesus' miracles who even "trusted in his name." Yet their lack of saving trust is clear for it says that Jesus did not entrust himself to them. He knew all men; he knew what was in a man. In John 8:31-59 we see again a group of people described as believers yet who do not hold to Christ's teaching; they end up trying to stone him!

5. The Enlightened Jews (Heb. 6:4-9)—These people experienced the influence of God's Spirit but not his saving influence. What is said of them (that "they are crucifying the Son of God all over again and subjecting him to public disgrace," and that it is impossible for them "to be brought back to repentance") cannot be said of a true Christian. In verse 9 the writer shifts his address to those who are Christians: "Even though we speak like this, dear friends, we are confident of better things in your case—things that accompany salvation."

6. The Lordship People (Mt. 7:21-23)—These professors seem to have it all. Not only do they confess the lordship of Christ, they do so fervently. Their theology and piety seem sound. They manifest spiritual power by prophecy, driving out demons and performing miracles. But their *wills* have not been converted. Their lack of true regeneration is evident because Christ consigns them to hell as evildoers.

Clearly, we have sufficient warning both from our experiences with others and in Scripture that a partial response to the gospel is not only dangerous but prevalent. We should be cautious in identifying outwardly favorable reactions with regeneration. *Inquirer* or *seeker* is a more lucid and helpful way to denote people who indicate an interest in the gospel.

What an awful thought that many will come before Christ thinking they are included, and yet find they are excluded. We cannot shirk our responsibility to encourage people to "examine yourselves to see whether you are in the faith; test yourselves" (2 Cor. 13:5). They need a confrontation in love not a spiritual novelty derived from someone else's experience. They need salvation. We can turn them to the beatitudes, the first letter of John and to Psalm 51, urging them to read these and ask God to show them where they stand with him. This is biblical self-examination using that aspect of God's law that gives the evidences for new life. It differs from morbid introspection in that you use an objective criterion and avoid wallowing in subjective analysis.

What then are we trusting God to do? What do we mean when we say the whole gospel is for the whole personality? To respond adequately to these questions we need to examine the faculties comprising our personality. We also need to see how an imbalance can result when any one of these faculties is not touched by the Spirit of God.

5

The Whole Gospel
to the Mind:
Not Intellectualism but
Using Truth to Inform
and Humble the Mind

I made a courtesy call to the chaplain's office while visiting a college in the East. I was greeted by a big smile and warm handshake. We talked amiably about our concern for ministering to students and the needs of the campus. The Bible, Christ and witness were all words falling naturally from his lips. I was excited to meet a Christian with this calling. All the right bells seemed to be ringing as he said the words I wanted to hear.

All Head Knowledge
Later that day, I investigated the programs he was offering. I talked with students who knew him. Some questions were raised in my mind, so I returned to ask the chaplain about his own beliefs. Although somewhat taken aback by my boldness, he agreed in a condescending way to respond. Having grown up in an evangelical Christian home, he had always wanted to help people. He

felt the role of a clergyman would give him the most freedom from supervision and stereotypes to influence others in developing their potential.

At one of the leading liberal seminaries in the East he had "come of age" and repudiated the naiveté of his evangelical roots. The Bible was a source book of the "faith of the early church," and the Judeo-Christian tradition one of many valid expressions of the human search for the ultimate. Jesus? Well, he was an enlightened man, but you had to peel away the myths and legends that had grown up around him to find the "real" Jesus.

I walked away from that chaplain's office saddened to know the truth about a man with religious knowledge but no personalizing or proclaiming of the truths of the gospel. I had poured my interpretation into the words he used as mere symbols.

Unfortunately, this is not an isolated example. Often Christians think they have led someone to Christ, but in fact the person was only giving the answers the Christian wanted to hear.

The opposite extreme, however, is equally dangerous.

Little Head Knowledge
In my ministry to college students, I have the opportunity to welcome freshmen into the world of the college campus. I remember one fellow who seemed happy to meet other "Jesus people," as he called us. His enthusiasm was contagious. Later I found that his initial encounters with Christ and previous Christian fellowship were in a milieu that distrusted and despised the mind. Spontaneity, authenticity, joy, openness in relationships were the hallmarks of the group in which he was nurtured. But there was not much Bible teaching.

In hardly a month he was missing from our fellowship and was not in any other Christian group. He didn't have time to study the Scriptures, and when he did, he had the habit of opening the Bible anywhere, looking for a "blessing."

He had enthroned vivid, firsthand, emotional experiences as the criteria and content of faith. Now at college he met others with a variety of experiences and opinions that were not even close to Christianity.[1] But their experiences were just as intense. Why was his "religious trip" any more valid? they asked. Before long he was openly denying the faith and continues to do so to this day.

He had never really been converted for he did not make truth the criterion of experience. There was no submission of his rebellious mind to the authority of Scripture or his thoughts to the review of higher thoughts.[2] If the *content* of the gospel is Jesus Christ, the *intention* of the gospel is to bind the mind of the unbeliever to the authority of the New Testament and to the lordship of Jesus Christ. These are not two separate entities. The New Testament is the Word of our Lord; and, therefore, one of the signs of saving faith is a willingness to keep his teachings (1 Jn. 2:3-5).[3]

The Balance: Thinking God's Thoughts not Judging God's Ways

Briefly, the biblical teaching on the mind is that our mind is neither to be by-passed in our Christian faith nor is it to be ultimately trusted. Our mind is God-given. John Stott puts it this way:

> Our rationality is part of the divine image. . . . To deny our rationality is therefore to deny our humanity, to become less than human beings. Scripture forbids us to behave like horses or mules which are "without understanding" and commands us instead in our understanding to be "mature." . . . Many imagine that faith is entirely irrational. But Scripture never sets faith and reason over against each other as incompatible. On the contrary, faith can only arise and grow within us by the use of our minds. "Those who know thy name put their trust in thee"; their trust springs from their knowledge of the trustworthiness of God's character. Again, "Thou dost keep him in perfect peace, whose mind is stayed on thee, because he trusts in thee." Here trusting in God and staying the mind on God are synonyms, and perfect peace is the result."[4]

The Fall has infected our minds so that, apart from the Spirit, they cannot come to the right conclusions morally. They do not interpret "facts" (evidence) as God does. The proper function of the mind is to think God's thoughts after him. The improper use is to sit in judgment upon God and his ways. Our minds are not "neutral"; they will not naturally respond and follow the truth of the gospel though they may still operate on certain principles of rationality such as the law of contradiction. They suppress moral implications of the truth (Rom. 1:18). They are at enmity with God (Rom. 8:7). As fallen men and women, we must repent of the desire to be mentally autonomous. We must cast down our vain imaginings and proud thoughts of ourselves. None of us will be called who *continues* in his own wisdom.

Os Guinness tells a rather humorous story which illustrates this truth. A man walked into a psychiatrist's office one day insisting he was dead. After several sessions with this "dead" man, the psychiatrist at last thought he had hit upon a solution to his patient's problem. He assigned him to go to the library and write an extensive paper on the characteristics of dead people. The doctor did not hear from him for several months. Then one day he received in the mail a large manuscript, the fruit of his patient's labors on this topic. One of his main conclusions was the interesting fact that dead people do not bleed. Overjoyed, the psychiatrist called the man in for an appointment. As soon as the man arrived, he began once again to proclaim that he was dead. At that moment the doctor whipped out a large hat pin and pricked the man's finger. Blood rushed out profusely. "There now, what conclusion do you draw from that?" asked the doctor. After a moment's hesitation, yet without blinking, the patient looked the doctor straight in the eye, and exclaimed, "Well, what do you know; dead people do bleed after all!"

Likewise, in spite of all the evidence, the minds of sinful men and women cling to twisted views like a child clutching a favorite toy. We change all evidence to fit our presuppositions.

We are not in any way, however, to encourage non-Christians to put their minds on the shelf in considering the claims of Christ. We invite them to use their minds. " 'Come now, and let us reason together,' says the Lord" (Is. 1:18).[5] Paul disputed or argued. He used logic. He did everything possible to clarify and to help unbelievers understand. The apostles used educational evangelism. Indeed, the very vehicle by which God gave his revelation—*words* —assumes engagement with our minds.

So in witnessing to the whole person we should use methods that communicate to the mind. Admittedly, our culture (and worse yet, some parts of the church) rely on another approach to influence people by distracting the mind so that it can be by-passed. (Francis Schaeffer uses the illustration of the burglar who uses meat to distract the dog while he goes about his real business of robbery.) Thus elections are won, products sold and converts produced by creating a pleasing image and obtaining an uncritical response—rather than by reasonably discussing issues or merits.

We must eschew any kind of evangelism that either overly exalts the mind or unduly neglects it.

6

The Whole Gospel to the Emotions:
Not Emotionalism but Showing Love and Touching the Heart

Jill sat next to me crying—and I never carry a handkerchief in church! I overheard someone say it had been a "powerful" service. It was over now, and I sat with my friend in the pew trying to recall the meeting. One of those testifying had choked up and was unable to finish. Then the preacher started in on the love of God. Why, you'd be a fool not to respond.

Only Emotional Reaction
My friend Jill then broke into my recollections. "How did he know how much I want to be loved? It seems he was speaking right to me. Everything I ever wanted he says Jesus will give me. . . . Then that long song at the end. The music just did something to me—and he kept pleading with us. After a while it got to me—how I'd messed my life up. I wanted to do something. I didn't want to disappoint the speaker so I raised my hand. Something, I'm not sure

what, was making me feel sorry, hopeful and confused all at once. I was so shaken I couldn't think straight about anything. I don't know what's happening to me."

Was Jill converted? What do you think? Let's look at the opposite end of the emotional spectrum.

No Emotional Reaction

"Well, that's the truth and you can take it or leave it." I'm not sure the preacher said exactly that, but that certainly was the impression he conveyed. His complacency and bored matter-of-factness permeated the entire sermon, and he ended it the same way—so abrupt, so cold. He spoke on Christ's love for sinners, but he gave no indication that he wanted people to respond. He showed no interest in his audience. There was no pleading with them to come to Christ. It reminded me of the student who approached me on campus and wanted to show me some little booklet. He was halfway through his presentation before he looked up at my face and saw that I wanted to speak. It was all so mechanical. So impersonal. So unreal. He also talked of a God of love, but I felt he didn't care at all about me.

The particular evangelical subculture in which we have been converted will often set the pattern for much of our subsequent growth, attitudes and view of spirituality. One subculture will bring forth emotionally stunted converts who often wear masks. They sometimes seem stiff, unnatural, embarrassed when the talk goes beyond clichés and into "what does this mean to you?" Another subculture has many who affect an exuberance that is all the more hollow. Perhaps they are trying to cover over what is lacking in their faith; maybe it's an unconscious mimic of what their group leaders convey as "spiritual." What can we do to safeguard our evangelism so that it does not run to either extreme of stoicism or emotionalism?

The Balance: Emotions Led by Truth

On the subject of emotions, evangelicals are schizophrenic. Some have been so threatened by the accusation of emotionalism that they backpedal as hard as they can. They fall into an unloving smugness. The religious publisher lauds the academic credentials of his writers or the Christian school president points to his large percentage of faculty with Ph.D.'s. Others have been so bored with the sterility of the lives of supposed believers that they rush forward, seeking experience after experience and follow anyone who exudes a warm glow. All evangelistic endeavors must be positive, peppy and have a leader who can "attract young people" (good looking, athletic and humorous). If you believe my analysis is extreme, I simply invite you to peruse some evangelical magazines and popular books, and visit churches and fellowship groups outside your normal circles.

Once again, we hold on to part of the truth while we are missing the beautiful balance of Scripture. Emotions are part of the image of God in us. If our feelings have been legitimately aroused, they should be expressed, not suppressed. Emotions have a valid place in our lives, but they are not to *lead* our lives. Truth is to lead, with emotions and will conforming. We must allow truth to grip us.

Nothing sets the heart on fire like truth. Truth is not cold and dry. On the contrary, it is warm and passionate. And whenever new vistas of God's truth open up to us, we cannot just contemplate. We are stirred to respond, whether to penitence or to anger or to love or to worship. Think of the two disciples walking to Emmaus on the first Easter afternoon while the risen Lord spoke to them. When He vanished, they said to each other, "Did not our hearts burn within us while He talked to us on the road, while He opened to us the Scriptures?" . . . What was the cause of their spiritual heartburn? It was Christ's opening the Scriptures to them! . . . As F. W. Faber once said, "Deep theology is the best fuel of devotion; it readily catches fire, and once kindled it burns long."[1]

Paul burst into an exhilarating doxology over doctrine! (Eph. 1:6-10). It is gratifying to see some new thinking by evangelicals on our emotions.[2] God made us in his image. He has emotions.

Let's quit denying ours!

In witnessing we must be emotional. How can we not? We're talking of the deepest *love* in the world. We're pressing on the conscience the awful *anger* of God against personal sin and social injustice. We're communicating the reconciling *peace* of God. Our theme is the liberating *joy* of no condemnation for those in Christ Jesus, the Jesus who *wept* over Jerusalem's unbelief. Have you? It is said that some of the Puritans stained the floor with their tears as they prayed. Is there pain and unceasing sorrow in our hearts for anyone who is yet unconverted? What if we do experience these emotions for sinners in private? Is it wholesome to expose them in public? *Very.*

One fall night in 1978 my wife, Suzanne, and I were at home together. The phone had rung several times with calls of one sort or another. I was beginning to become a little protective about my privacy. Just then the phone rang again. I reluctantly answered and heard the rough voice of an older man say, "Is this the Willie Metzger that used to live in Baltimore?"

"Yes," I replied with hesitation. When he called me "Willie," I knew this must be a voice out of the distant past. I was hoping that he wasn't going to keep me guessing. He didn't.

"Do you remember being on a busload of students headed for the IVCF Urbana Missionary Convention in Illinois in 1961?"

My reply was, "Of course." But I was not completely honest, for by now I had been to six of these triennial conventions, and they were becoming one blurred recollection. It was now seventeen years since that particular bus ride.

The gruff voice continued, "Well, I was the driver for that bus, and you stayed up during the overnight drive and talked with me about my family problems and about Jesus Christ. I was housed near the convention, and you even came by my room one night to ask me to come with you to a meeting. I refused and kept drinking my beer and watching TV. Then, on the long ride home you urged me to consider becoming a Christian. I was skeptical and cynical. How could a young kid like you know the solution to the hard problems of marriage and job and money that I was facing?''

At that point I broke in, ''Al! Yes, yes, I do remember you now. Go on.'' I listened intently as the bus driver told me how he had put the Bible and a note I had given him on his closet shelf together with a letter his dad had written him urging him to get right with God. Then, in the spring of 1978, he reached up to get his jacket from that closet shelf. There he found the Bible and the two letters. He took them down and began to read. His heart was softened. Later that summer he went to hear a gospel preacher at the invitation of his son.

''I really got converted,'' he said. ''Since we last met I've become a truck driver. You know, those big eighteen-wheelers on interstate hauls. I've miraculously survived two bad crashes. God kept after me all those years. I've been baptized and joined a little church here. My wife and others in my family are Christians too. I found your phone number in Baltimore written in that Bible. So I called up and your dad gave me your new number. I often thought of you, and I just wanted to let you know what's happened. I don't remember much of what you said to me back in 1961, but I remember your concern and sincerity, and I still have your note and the Bible. Keep loving people to the Lord, Willie, no matter how long it takes.''

We need to let our non-Christian friends know how we feel. Many of us are unemotional, numbed by our culture. We need verbally to affirm others as we see God's gifts to them. We should struggle to express to others that we love them. How well I remember the time when I knew I couldn't say anything more in a conversation with a younger relative. It seemed right to hug her, and the words came out, ''Oh, how I wish you'd become a Christian!'' On another occasion I was unconscious of the deep tone of concern that was coming through during an intense talk with an uncle of mine. He remarked that he hoped *I* would not suffer frustration and depression as a result of his unwillingness to be converted. He could see that I cared.

In witnessing we endeavor to touch the heart of unbelievers.

We want them to fall in love with Jesus. Isn't it the love of Christ that draws sinners? Let's allow for differences in the emotional make-up of people. But let's never forget to involve their emotions.

One word of caution. If you have an especially forceful personality and can talk people into most anything, beware of manipulating others. This is a grave danger in evangelism among children or with an emotionally unstable person. To treat children or anyone else as saved on the basis of emotional reactions without further evidence may actually hinder them from seeking God truly and may result in their becoming bored with the gospel. Enthusiasm is easier to generate than continued obedience.

I realize the difficulty in refraining from pronouncing my own two young boys "saved" when they say a spontaneous prayer, show interest in Bible stories or sing loudly "Jesus Loves Me." As their father, I am so excited to see them react emotionally to Christ. But are they converted? It is such a temptation to say yes, but are they acting out of conformity or from the heart? Only time and the tests of life will tell. It is only when we face a choice in which our will must be overridden in order to do the will of Christ that we have insight into the reality of our salvation.

7

The Whole Gospel to the Will:
Not Appealing to Natural Desires but Inviting, Persuading and Demanding Allegiance to a New Master

The desire for success and status is strong. Sometimes the church feeds it instead of calling it by its true name—pride. Here's part of a letter written by a pastor to a young person going through a period of depression.

Only a Challenge
I'm writing to help you shake this feeling of uselessness that has overtaken you. Several times you have said that you don't see how Christ can possibly use you—that you're nobody special.

The church must bear part of the responsibility for making you feel as you do. I have in mind the success-story mentality of the church. Our church periodicals tell the story of John J. Moneybags who uses his influential position to witness for Christ. At the church youth banquet we have a testimony from All-American football star Ox Kickoffski, who commands the respect of his teammates when he witnesses for Christ. We've led you to think that if you don't have the leverage of stardom or a big position in the business world, you might as well keep your mouth shut . . . nobody cares what Christ has done for you.[1]

In addition, we make appeals stressing the "adventure of the Christian life," or we say, "Try Jesus because things go better with him." These are direct appeals to the will couched in terms of an exciting challenge. People get the impression that they can take up Jesus the same way they would take up jogging! These are attempts to trigger the will of a person by appeal to his or her human desires. It becomes a what's-in-it-for-me gospel.

No Persuasion

On the other end of the spectrum, I've met people whose story goes like this:

I had been putting off getting serious with God for quite a while. I enjoyed my Christian friends, and I knew I didn't have what they had; but I just didn't want to face up to becoming a Christian. It was kind of easy just to slide along with the meetings. Nobody ever really put me on the spot about my salvation. Now that I am a Christian, I wish someone had confronted me earlier. I needed to hear that it was something I shouldn't put off.

Or like this:

I'm not ready yet to come to God. My motives are so selfish. Besides, I don't understand enough yet. I want all my questions answered first. My pastor once said we really had to feel our guilt before we were ready for God's grace. I want to prepare myself more and come to God in just the right way. The pastor encouraged me to wait for God to move me. He didn't try to persuade me at all.

The Balance: God Moving Sinners through Persuasion

It is a mistake to appeal to the unbeliever's will directly if we do not accompany such an appeal with biblical content. Why? Because such content is needed to instruct the mind in its choice and humble its sinful desires.[2] It is possible to encourage unbelievers to arrive at decisions from false motives. They "become Christians" for what they can get out of it, such as coveting the speaker's experience or happiness or success in life. The true reason for becoming a Christian is not that we may have a wonderful life but that we may be in a right relationship to God. Too many of our evangelistic methods are benefit oriented. Phrases like "the adventure of the Christian life"; "the thrill and excitement"; "Christ made me happy every day" and so on, are not balanced with the cost of discipleship. "The most serious of all dangers is that of seeking to produce decisions as a result of pressure brought to bear upon the listener's will."[3] There is the danger of using our personality or stories to force listeners to respond to our appeal. Truth has neither convinced nor convicted them. Music can produce the same effect. People can so sing a chorus that eventually they become intoxicated. There is truth and value in such things as music to accompany evangelism, but they should not take the supreme and first position. They are aids and helps—not what actually produces the results.

On the other hand, Scripture does appeal to the will. It is no laissez-faire approach. "Choose for yourselves this day whom you will serve" (Josh. 24:15). "Come, all you who are thirsty, come to the waters" (Is. 55:1). "Come to me, all you who are weary and burdened" (Mt. 11:28). "Believe in the Lord Jesus, and you will be saved" (Acts 16:31). True evangelists *do* pop the question. In fact, we are to plead, command, invite and beg! It is uncomfortable for us when we put people on the spot, yet we must not neglect to call for a response. I can recall times when I have struggled to do this.

I have found myself saying, "This is really important; you ought to make up your mind. Perhaps you feel like I'm pressing you, but I only want to reflect the pressure of God's Spirit who is calling you to respond. If you feel in your conscience the force of truth as contained in Christ (not just because you don't want to disappoint me), then do surrender your whole life to him." Our sobering words may bring spiritual conviction to people. We want them to face God now, for it is a matter of life or death. There is to be a note of urgency and persuasion in our voice.

The sermons of great evangelists like Bunyan, Whitefield, Edwards and Spurgeon were all marked by direct questions and pleas put to unbelievers. Their personal witnessing was too. We are told in the autobiography of Spurgeon of a woman who had come to him several times for counsel. She had seen her need of Christ after listening to his sermons and wanted further instruction on how to become a Christian. Spurgeon tediously went over the gospel with her on each occasion. She would always end the session with, "Mr. Spurgeon, please pray for me." Spurgeon became exasperated and finally said, "Lady, pray for yourself, for I will not." This shocked her so much that she sought God directly and was soon converted.

There are astounding benefits that of course do come to believers (heaven assured, forgiveness, joy, love and peace). Nonbelievers can only desire these things in a selfish way, so we should not convey to them the idea of waiting until they have the right motives for coming to Christ. They never will, simply because they *cannot*. Sinners have the warrant to come *now*.

Let not conscience make you linger,
  Nor of fitness fondly dream;
All the fitness He requireth
  Is to feel your need of Him. . . .
Come, ye weary, heavy laden,
  Bruised and broken by the Fall;
If you tarry till you're better,
  You will never come at all.[4]

The Labeling Fallacy

This matter of the will and our need to call for a response is an especially sensitive area among evangelicals because of certain theological assumptions. There are those who are theologically self-conscious and concerned to define carefully every aspect of their evangelism. They remind me of the saying, "After all is said and done, there is more said than done!" They so fear doing anything unscriptural that they resist anything new and different. A desire to be scriptural is commendable; but if taken to an extreme, it is bondage to the letter and not the spirit of the law. It is one thing to hold strongly to your principles; it is another thing to fall into an overly scrupulous application of a principle in mechanical fashion. Such is bondage to tradition or to a pastor or to a principle —but not to the Lord. We must not be merely orthodox thinkers but Spirit-motivated doers.

Other evangelicals are theologically ignorant of why they do certain things in calling for a response to the gospel. These evangelicals should be willing to examine their theology. Instead of blindly imbibing a certain approach to the will evolved from unbiblical assumptions, they should critically look for the doctrinal basis of their methods. Evangelists should be more self-conscious of their theology for the sake of their own ministry and for their followers. Too many organizations and churches "do evangelism" a certain way only because "that's the way we've always done it." As the years go by, there is less and less examination of the theological basis for a particular method. As a result, people are loyal to a certain approach and not to the Scriptures. This breeds snobbish Christians. I'll never forget the reply given to me by a student when I asked about his style of evangelism. "I picked it up from my staff worker who told me this is the way our group has always done it on campus." When pressed further he could give no scriptural reasons for his method of evangelism. This did not make him any less certain, though, that "the people in the other Christian groups were doing it all wrong."

Labels are deadly in Christian circles. For example, when it comes to the topic of the will, immediately certain views are categorized as Reformed or Arminian. The discussion then ends because it is thought (wrongly) that as soon as you have given a name to something, you understand it. Instead, there should be continued dialog in the Scriptures by all of us. Let's fight this labeling fallacy. What exactly underlies these views on the will?

One view is that the Fall has only weakened the will of sinners and that we have the potential (or ability) to believe. This seems to provide a basis for appealing to unbelievers to respond, thus safeguarding the scriptural doctrine of human responsibility. In practice this view may lead to approving any method that evokes the latent potential to believe. This is the man-centered approach. Beginning with a well-meaning desire (sinners are responsible and should be urged to believe), an unwarranted conclusion is reached —since people are commanded to believe, they must have the ability.

The other view sees clearly that the will is dead in trespasses and sins. There is none that does good (Rom. 3). This honors God's initiative in salvation and establishes grace; but if the will is in bondage, some may hesitate to make an appeal for all people to believe. Beginning with a desire to exalt God, what seems to be a logical (but not scriptural) conclusion is drawn.

Both views have at least this in common: as a result of trying to be faithful to Scripture, you might begin with either view and go beyond Scripture, not keeping the doctrines of divine sovereignty and human responsibility in balance.

The writers of the Bible are not embarrassed to put side by side teachings that do not fit our logic.[5] For example, Peter charges his hearers on the day of Pentecost with wickedness in killing Christ, yet admits it was all in God's plan (Acts 2:23). Paul tells the sailors that God has promised no one will be lost in the storm, yet warns them to stay on the boat or they will perish (Acts 27: 22, 31). Jesus says, "No one can come to me unless the Father who sent me draws him." Yet, "Whoever comes to me I will never drive away," also is true (Jn. 6:37, 44). How can this be? To our finite minds such teachings seem to be at odds with each other. We try and try to reconcile them. Perhaps we should not consider these two doctrines of sovereignty and responsibility as enemies, but rather, see them the way the Bible does—as friends!

Man-centered theology is man-pleasing (centering on the ability, potential, capacity of fallen man) and takes human responsibility to an extreme. Its historical basis is found in the work of Pelagius in the fifth century and later the writings of Jacobus Arminius (1560-1609) who reacted against a wrong emphasis he felt existed in the churches of Holland. Arminius thought the creeds accepted in the church of Holland denied that humans are responsible for their moral actions, and indeed the preaching in the churches may have neglected this aspect of Scripture. So, his followers taught that divine sovereignty is not compatible with human responsibility and that human ability limits our obligation.[6]

Horrified by the implications of this teaching, the church synod re-emphasized God's sovereignty in salvation (sinners do not save themselves or contribute to their salvation in any way), insisting it was a work of grace from beginning to end. Five statements were formulated in reaction to five articles proposed by the Arminians. We make a mistake, therefore, if we consider the five points of this synod to be a balanced creedal statement. The "five points of Calvinism" as these later became known are orthodox theology, but are in need of further filling out with the whole counsel of God because they are merely a reaction to a theological distortion. A scriptural emphasis on divine sovereignty and human responsibility should be at the heart of a right view of the human will and a recovery of the gospel in our day. In witnessing we trust in the inherent power of "the word and the Spirit"; we speak to sinners, and by this God-ordained means, the God-ordained end is accomplished. God has ordained both the means and the end.

Reaching the Whole Person

To analyze human nature I have divided it into the three segments of mind, heart and will. But these are only aspects of a unified human personality; I do not mean to leave the impression that these are independent of each other.[7]

People cannot give a holistic response. Because sin has brought fragmentation we are not whole people. The way in which people come to Christ will vary depending on how sin has incapacitated them (it may have a stronger hold on one aspect than another) and on their unique temperaments. Some will lead with their emotions, letting their minds catch up later. A cerebral person, on the other hand, may have difficulty responding emotionally. And people today seldom use their will in making decisions because our sensuous culture influences them to react according to their desires.

At the same time, I do not intend to say that people can make a proper response to Christ on one level but not on the others. The mind, heart and will are all involved to some extent in every action. Our evangelism must therefore be to the whole person, allowing that the response will be in accord with each unique personality.

May God grant that as we direct unbelievers to Christ we shall see more and more wholly converted people, people of whom we can say, "But thanks be to God that, though you used to be slaves to sin, you wholeheartedly [from the center of your being] obeyed [will] the form of teaching [mind] to which you were entrusted" (Rom. 6:17). Directing people to trust in Christ alone can be hard work. It requires boldness and keeping our eye on pleasing God not others.

Hundreds of years ago John Bunyan commended this ministry of "faithful dealing" with men who are merely talkers, having no true faith.

> You did well to talk so plainly to him as you did. There is but little of this faithful dealing with men now-a-days, and that makes religion to stink in the nostrils of many as it doth; for they are these talkative fools whose religion is only in word, and are debauched and vain in their conversation (conduct), that (being much admitted into the fellowship of the godly) do stumble the world, blemish Christianity, and grieve the sincere. I wish that all men would deal with such as you have done: then should they either be made more conformable to religion, or the company of saints would be too hot for them.[8]

One result of theologically examining regeneration and saving faith has been to change the personal testimony of some, including me. I now understand my initial interest in Jesus Christ as the beginning of my awakening and not my conversion. I find myself dating my conversion much later, though I still don't know the day. I now think of my conversion as closer to a time when I began to understand who Jesus was. As my life slowly took on a new direction, I had assurance of salvation. This new insight into what God was doing in my life seems to coincide with scriptural teaching. I would suggest we ask two questions to people who have made a profession of faith and have come to us for counsel:

"What has Christ done *for* you?" (Is there an objective understanding of the main content of the gospel?)[9]

"What has Christ done *in* you?" (Is there any evidence of new life, a changed heart?)

Part III

Offered by Whole People: Character and Communication in Witnessing

For the appeal we make does not spring from error or impure motives, nor are we trying to trick you. On the contrary, we speak as men approved by God to be entrusted with the gospel. We are not trying to please men but God, who tests our hearts. You know we never used flattery, nor did we put on a mask to cover up greed—God is our witness. We were not looking for praise from men, not from you or anyone else.

As apostles of Christ we could have been a burden to you, but we were gentle among you, like a mother caring for her little children. We loved you so much that we were delighted to share with you not only the gospel of God but our lives as well, because you had become so dear to us. Surely you remember, brothers, our toil and hardship; we worked night and day in order not to be a burden to anyone while we preached the gospel of God to you.

You are witnesses, and so is God, of how holy, righteous and blameless we were among you who believed. For you know that we dealt with each of you as a father deals with his own children, encouraging, comforting and urging you to live lives worthy of God, who calls you into his kingdom and glory.
1 Thessalonians 2:3-12

8

The Normal Christian Evangelist

Our age emphasizes the how-to, the do-it-yourself, and the instant—the enthronement of the pragmatic and practical. This can be a healthy counterbalance to absorption in theoretical talk. We can become so concerned with understanding what to do that we never get around to *doing* it! We've talked about witnessing; the question now is, with what individuals are *you* involved? Will you do-it-yourself?

The Need for a Method
In part one I set forth the need for a recovery of the gospel. Part two emphasized the need to reinstate the goal of complete conversion. In this section we are exploring the need to restore a connection between biblical knowledge about evangelism and the actions that result from and are compatible with that knowledge. Action should be the fruit of sound doctrine.

Why is it necessary to consider how we present the gospel? Lloyd-Jones contends that we cannot assume that those who believe the right way will necessarily present that belief in the right way.[1] Some Christians who are orthodox believers cannot point to a fruitful work. On the other hand, some seem to get phenomenal results, but those results do not last. Lloyd-Jones explains that these two extremes both result from a gap between what a person believes and what he or she actually teaches. We all need to re-examine our evangelism to make sure that we do not simply talk *about* the gospel or that we are so interested in applying the gospel (getting results) that we slight the theological content.

There was a time when I would have avoided any mention of approaches or techniques to use to present the gospel. Now I see this was an overreaction to the abuses of method-centered evangelism. As I have labored both to be a more faithful witness myself and to train others, I see an undeniable need for good training materials.

It is all well and good for Christians to speak of relational skills and say, "True witnessing is the overflow of a full life. You can't train someone to witness—it's out of character with the whole idea of witnessing." Yes, Jesus Christ should just spill over from our lives. But is witnessing only something we *are?* The Christians I see emphasizing this approach usually have great relational and verbal skills, while most of us do not.

Again and again as I meet Christians eager to witness, I find them asking for help: "How do I start? What do I say?" I agree that you can find no set witnessing techniques in the ministry of our Lord. But we are not like him—yet. So we must start with would-be Christian evangelists where they are if we want to help them to witness. As we have seen, this involves instruction in gospel theology. They also need seedling methods for how to relate this truth content to non-Christians. We must ask ourselves, What kind of evangelism training will produce a natural and spontaneous communication of Jesus and ourselves? I feel our ability to witness begins with a big view of God and Jesus that will give young Christians a basis for being confident, expectant and comfortable with their humanity. Then we can show that the truth of the gospel frees people for it has freed us to live differently and speak with conviction (Jn. 8:32). As we speak God's Word we have the promise that our witness is not in vain (Is. 55:11).

Relational evangelism, in spite of its good intentions, does not put its emphasis on the hearing of the word of truth as the necessary kindling which the Holy Spirit ignites in regeneration (Rom. 10:17). Relational evangelism's approach can neglect the theological content of the gospel by shifting the focus to the personality and experience of the evangelist. God intends us to be witnesses and has empowered us by the Holy Spirit (Acts 1:8). In our calling to be Exhibit A, not only are we to live our joy but we are also to explain the ingredients of the gospel. Receiving the ingrafted word brings salvation (Jas. 1:21).

As we follow Jesus' exhortation to fish for men, we not only need a knowledge of the nature of the fish (the unbelievers) and the nature of our bait (the gospel), but we also need to understand how to use a fishing line! A fisherman selects a proper weight, line and hook according to what he is trying to catch. The novice must learn by rote certain methods and principles, which sooner or later will become second nature. So too, we need help in choosing methods appropriate to our message and to our audience. May we as fishers of men also find our fishing becoming second nature.

The problem of "dropout" from evangelism has been much debated.[2] We will never eliminate it. Yet, we should not stop trying, for this is part of being faithful to our calling. The honor of our Savior demands as clear and balanced a witness as possible. Our high view of witnessing derives from our high view of God. Our witness should be consistent with our worship. Yet never are we to trust in the accuracy of our theological expression of the gospel.

What follows are some suggestions that have been helpful for me and others who desire to witness. Of course, they can be used in the wrong way. We need to pray that God will take away any timidity and give us a spirit of power, love and discernment. Nothing works automatically. As we obey Jesus' command to speak of him to others, he will help us find a method that is compatible to our personality.[3]

Our Fears

Evangelism is not just for the super-Christian; the Bible is clear that all real Christians have this privilege (Acts 8:1, 4; 2 Cor. 5: 18-20). I could have said "responsibility" instead of privilege, but our personal experience of sovereign and free grace turns duty into love, responsibility into privilege. Some may have gifts which especially suit them to this task—facility of speech, ease of meeting people and so on. Yet, if we think we possess no "gift of evangelism," we could come to the false conclusion that we have no responsibility to witness. I am not sure what the gift of evangelism is, but I have a feeling that with God's help *many* people can be gifted in this area, since all are called to witness.

If we lack this desire that comes from a heart overflowing with gratitude to the Lord, then we should ask God whether or not we have experienced salvation.

Much has been written and said to try to motivate Christians to witness. Later I will mention some reasons why our motivation is often weak. Actually, if people do not have the desire, there is no use trying to train them. We might try, instead, giving them a strong dose of teaching on justification by faith. Unmerited mercy softens cold hearts.

Even motivated Christians, however, will have misgivings as they witness. The basis of these apprehensions is fear.

What kind of person has God called us to be as we seek to love and instruct others in the gospel? He wants us to be ourselves. People do not just hear syllables from our mouths; they pick up connotations from our lives. Even our body speaks. Body language (eye contact, stance, hand movements) indicates our interest or disinterest, our patience or impatience. If we are nervous, we will make others uncomfortable too.

Do you convey a proud I-have-it-and-you-don't spirit? Remind yourself that God's favor toward you is totally unmerited. Are you afraid of mentioning Christ? One of God's servants had to be reminded who had made his mouth (Ex. 4:11). Another was told not to be ashamed (2 Tim. 1:8). You are no better nor worse than they —just a sinner saved by grace. How about your own ignorance and doubts? A sovereign God knows all this. Don't you realize he will give you the words and will teach you to trust?

We may feel insecure because we're not sure how people will respond to our message. But we need to face the fact that our gospel is unavoidably offensive to unbelievers. It is the gospel of a crucified Savior. As Paul points out in 1 Corinthians 1, it is a stumbling block and foolishness to others. It makes *exclusive* claims on its followers in our culture of religious syncretism. The "dirty words" that offend the modern mind are concepts like: a God who holds absolute sway over our destiny; a God who will hold us accountable for our behavior; a God whose Son is the only person who can sign us up in the book of life; a God who says we must humble ourselves and base our hope on the righteousness of a substitute.

We can also overcome our insecurity by looking to Christ not others. I have not always been willing to admit this inherent offensiveness and thus bear the misunderstanding and mockery of others. I would either be silent about the faith, or I would try to paint it up so well that Christ couldn't help but be attractive. My reason was poor—I didn't want to look like a fool! My security and self-image desperately needed the acceptance of my peers. I was afraid of what they might think of me.

I remember returning home after my first year away at college, anxious to practice what I had learned about witnessing. A close friend of mine to whom I have never said anything about Christ had also just returned from his first year away. I carefully planned an afternoon of swimming so that Dick and I could be alone and talk. Here was the ideal situation for witnessing—and do you know what happened? I never brought up the subject! I felt so badly that night as I confessed my insecurities to God. Later I wrote a long letter to Dick at school. I was finding out the truth that "fear of man will prove to be a snare" (Prov. 29:25).

Our weaknesses can become the means through which God works in evangelism. Both the Old and New Testaments describe how God's ministry was carried out by very ordinary people. God met them in their weakness. Jeremiah was young and fearful (Jer. 1:4-9), and Paul had to learn that his weakness was a plus factor (2 Cor. 12:9-10). Turn your weakness into an asset by owning it in a way that produces humility. (See appendix B, worksheet 3.)

God goes before us in each encounter with unbelievers. Knowing him, the God who initiates salvation, calms our fears and removes any reason for timidity or manipulation in a relationship. Along with humility, we can have the other necessary characteristic for witness: boldness. The New Testament evangelists are frequently described as bold (Acts 4:13, 29; 14:3; Eph. 6:19-20; 1 Thess. 1:5; 2:2). Boldness in prayer preceded boldness in witnessing. We discover we are not to confront people with ourselves but with the risen Christ—placing them in his presence.[4]

Batman and Robin on the Beach

During spring break thousands of college students flock to Florida for the "Four S" experience: sun, surf, sex, and suds (foaming beer). A number of years back I was part of Inter-Varsity Christian Fellowship's beach evangelism team one spring. After spending the daylight hours striking up conversations on the beach and preaching from under a large orange umbrella, I decided to scout out where the students went at night.

I soon discovered one old motel in the area that was crammed with beds. Arms and legs hung out the screenless windows. I asked the owner if he would mind if our group used the courtyard to play some guitars and try to talk to the students. As you can imagine, anything we wanted to do "to help these crazy kids" was all right with him. I began to lay my plans.

The next night at dusk I returned with my partners. It didn't help me much that one of my helpers was Paul Little, experienced evangelist and author of many books on the subject. He thought it would be a good idea for *me* to give the talk after we had drawn a crowd by some singing. Looking back on it now, I wonder at my eagerness.

It only took a few minutes for us to realize that things were not going to go our way that night. We were up against two factors we had not considered. First, I had not noticed there was no electric light in the courtyard. Second, since it had rained all day the students had not gone out to the beach but stayed in their rooms. As a result, their drinking had begun about noon. Unfortunately, it was only *after* I stood up on a picnic table to speak that I realized how dark it was and how drunk they were! I also noticed for the first time the high brick wall that I was backed up against.

Not five minutes into my talk, a heckler shouted a question. When I suggested he hold his question until the end, another voice in the crowd took it upon himself to shout an answer. A loud argument ensued between two people whom I couldn't even see. I continued to try to finish my talk. Another question was shouted at me, and then another. Paul, sensing things were a little out of hand, whispered to me that I should walk over and talk to one of the questioners. He would take the other. This dispersed the crowd and all the curiousity seekers left. As one of the students was walking away I heard him ask another in a disgusted voice, "Hey, who are those two guys?" The reply that came was in slurred speech, "Oh, it's just Batman and Robin, the boy wonder," pointing a beer can at us.

It will take boldness to speak of Christ to strangers. Yet often more boldness will be needed to face friends and family than an unruly mob.

Wholeness in Attitudes and Motivation

Following the command to make disciples will become the mechanical performance of a duty unless we have had an inward experience of Jesus discipling us. We can only talk about the things we have seen and heard (Acts 4:20). God's *command* to make disciples and our experience of *his love* that speaks from within combine with the desperate *need of others*. These are the three truths that motivate us.[5]

Why then is lack of motivation often a problem? There can be many reasons. If there is unconfessed and unforsaken sin, it would be well to study Psalm 51. Be sure, however, to distinguish between true guilt (breaking God's standard) and environmental guilt (going against the customs of others, even the customs of evangelical Christians containing manmade ideas of witnessing). If we are waiting for that inner urge before we tell someone the gospel, it will probably never come. Our feelings were not meant to determine our actions. God calls us to obedience not waiting for a feeling. Selfishness is often at the root of our nonwitness. We do not want to be troubled. Sometimes inexperience or perhaps a bad experience in witnessing can account for a lack of motivation. We can ask a friend to share his or her witnessing experiences and we can join together in some new attempts. A desire to witness is often caught from another.

We must be ourselves in our evangelism. We need to be honest and admit our hang-ups. How many times have nonbelievers not talked with Christians because they thought the believers were unreal? "You just couldn't understand because you never seem to have any problems." Honesty is often the opening to genuine witness. Why not? Are you afraid God's reputation will be tarnished? God grant us a healthy self-forgetfulness at times. It's in the setting of our weakness that the gem of God's strength is reflected. We need to be real, be whole.

Do we love others? Translated into practical terms, "How much time do I give to others? Do I spend time only with people who are like me? What do I enjoy most? Would I forgo it to help someone? Am I constantly thinking only of my time, fun and interests? Love is enterprising and has an inventive genius all its own. Gratitude for God's grace and a love for Christ spontaneously overflow to those around us. "Why is it that we who have assumed the name of the compassionate one are so lacking in compassion? . . . Without compassion, witness in all its varied forms is ineffective, flaccid, and at times obnoxious. . . . If you are going to involve yourself in the lives and problems of others, you will get your heart broken. You will have to suffer yourself—and not just a little bit! Involvement will mean real personal sacrifice."[6] Our heart must be set on the salvation of others. When this end is not reached, we will be deeply pained. Complacency is a sign of an indifference to even our own salvation. When have we been "moved with compassion" like our Lord or, like Paul, cried out with our hearts for the salvation of others (Mk. 6:34; Rom. 9:1-3)?

The glue for Christlike friendship is loyalty and faithfulness. With our culture becoming increasingly mobile (one out of every four people moves each year) and fractured (the family, the last model of loyalty and security, is fading), most people end up being very self-centered. Opposed to this is the biblical picture of love. Think what the following words might mean in a friendship with a non-Christian. (See appendix B, worksheet 6.)

This love of which I speak is slow to loose patience—it looks for a way of being constructive. It is not possessive: it is neither anxious to impress nor does it cherish inflated ideas of its own importance.

Love has good manners and does not pursue selfish advantage. It is not touchy. It does not keep account of evil or gloat over the wickedness of other people. On the contrary, it shares the joy of those who live by the truth.

Love knows no limit to its endurance, no end to its trust, no fading of its hope; it can outlast anything. (1 Cor. 13:4-7 Phillips)

The supreme motive in witnessing is to glorify God, to see his perfections manifested through the joyous praises of his redeemed people. If in our heart of hearts this is not our driving force, if our witness is ruled by a lesser motive, we are out of harmony with the plan of salvation. The great aim of divine election is glorification of God (Rom. 11:36; Eph. 1:12). If we proclaim Christ without this master motive, we work at cross-purposes with both our message and with the Spirit.[7]

In speaking to the Thessalonians, Paul could point to himself
and his companions as whole people (1 Thess. 2:1-12). Their
evangelistic methods were exemplary. Coming in weakness,
suffering and at sacrifice to themselves, these evangelists spoke
the Word of God boldly yet amid much opposition. They exhorted
others with authority and could boast that their witness did not
originate in error, impurity or deceit. Likewise, we are not to be
men-pleasers, but God-pleasers—for God examines our motivation. Let's not manipulate his Word to bring people to Christ.
Let's not try to always look good. There should be no flattering
speech, no pretext for greed, no seeking of fame. Rather, we are to
have gentleness (like a nursing mother cares for her own) and a
fond affection, and to impart the gospel (solid truth content) and
our own lives (flesh-and-blood incarnation of the truth). Paul and
his fellow evangelists fell in love with these people and supported
themselves so as not to be a burden. They cared for them like a
father for his own children.[8]

Prayer and the Spirit
Prayer for others is the supreme God-ordained method in evangelism. Unless God changes a person's heart, nothing lasting will
be achieved. Prayer is a means of raising dead sinners to life! In
the Old Testament, we read of the effect of prayer: God "remem-
bered Abraham [his prayers], and he brought Lot out of the
catastrophe that overthrew the cities where Lot had lived" (Gen.
19:29). Until we see the incapacity of sinners and our helplessness to save them, we will not commit ourselves to pray; prayer
is pleading our helplessness before God.

We should have a sense of expectancy in our prayers. God is
willing and able to save a great number of people. We can rev-
erently remind God of his promise and his purpose to build a kingdom. God will use us. Christ has promised to make us fishers of
men.

We are to have a sense of longing as we pray. Paul said his

heart's desire and prayer to God for Israel was that they might be saved. He had unceasing anguish and sorrow for unbelievers. Paul told Agrippa boldly of his longing for Agrippa's conversion. Do we really *desire* others to be saved?

A hidden and deeply spiritual ministry of prayer is needed to back our evangelistic activity:

> God will make us pray before He blesses our labors in order that we may constantly learn afresh that we depend on God for everything. And then, when God permits us to see conversions, we shall not be tempted to ascribe them to our own gifts, or skill or wisdom, or persuasiveness, but to His work alone, and so we shall know whom we ought to thank for them. . . . "Pray for us," writes Paul to the Thessalonians, "that the word of the Lord may run and be glorified." Paul was a great evangelist who had seen much fruit, but Paul knew that every particle of it had come from God . . . This, to Paul, was an urgent request just because Paul sees so clearly that his preaching can save nobody unless God in sovereign mercy is pleased to bless it and use it to this end . . . Evangelistic fruitfulness [will not come] unless God also reforms our praying, and pours out in us a new spirit of supplication for evangelistic work.[9]

It is unfortunate that our mental image of an evangelist is often abnormal when compared with Scripture. Instead of our picture of a supersalesman who has stage presence and the gift of gab, we are to be merely humans at home with their Maker and themselves. God's evangelists are called to be whole (complete, real, balanced, integrated) people. God gives us his Spirit (the comforter) not to make us comfortable but to make us comforters of others.

9

How to Communicate Personally

What is appropriate in some situations and relationships is not appropriate in others. Usually we don't communicate in the same way to our parents as we do to a stranger. So also in expressing the gospel to parents and strangers we will normally see a difference in approach. Of course, the Holy Spirit leads us differently at times as well.

Different People, Different Places
I well remember the time I set up a display of Christian books for a fair at a large indoor shopping mall in Delaware. This would be a good time to catch up on my reading, I thought, because I was sure nothing much would happen. A stranger came by and within fifteen minutes told me some of his most personal problems. "I don't know why I'm telling you these things. I haven't even told my wife," he said. God's Spirit opened the way for a very direct

witness. Although he moved to a different city shortly thereafter, he followed my suggestion of reading the literature he bought and calling up a pastor. Now he and his family are in God's kingdom.

Normally, we proceed slowly with strangers and even more so with parents. We appreciate the zeal of a young convert who returns home to lecture to his parents on his new-found faith. Of course, what they *hear* him saying is, "You didn't raise me right. I reject you." We admire the zeal but can see it is ill-suited to the situation.

Jesus provides us with many examples of the different relationships he had with people. He made friends with sinners and witnessed to them (Zaccheus). He confronted religious people (Nicodemus). Although little is said about it, he certainly carried on a witness in his own home, family and neighborhood. Jesus also spoke to strangers. The remarkable story in John 4 of Jesus' encounter with a Samaritan woman at a well gives instructive lessons in personal witness. Jesus breaks through several barriers that often stop us cold. He speaks to a woman (sex and cultural barriers of the day), who is a Samaritan (religious and ethnic barriers). He is never condescending but rather asks help of her. Moving from a common concern on the physical level (water, thirst), he develops a conversation about spiritual matters. He never manipulates her nor compromises the truth. He brings her back to the central issue again and again. He is patient, he exposes her unspoken needs, and he speaks to her conscience. He reveals himself to her as Messiah.

Our relationships with others can be broken down into these categories:

Long-term intimate—such as family, close friends, roommate.

Long-term acquaintance—some relatives, neighbors, peers, people at school or work.

Short-term intimate—friends, business associates, classmates.

Short-term acquaintance—people met in passing: in a store, on a bus, at the beach.

Our approach in evangelism is probably different according to the relationship. Surely we have a unique responsibility to those in long-term relationships. These people know our faults, and our deeds may well have to precede any words of witness we can speak.

Where most of us need to see our responsibility, however, is in the area of short-term relationships. We don't take the initiative, so these people are often on their way without hearing anything from us. I believe we have a responsibility to such people. Some of us use our personalities to excuse ourselves for lack of witness in these passing situations: "I'm not an outgoing person, I could never speak to a stranger!" *All* of us are responsible to step out in faith in *all* of our relationships with people. The point is not that we feel comfortable in witnessing, but that we recognize God's sovereignty in bringing each person across our path.

If this sounds like theology, know that our theology is meant to prod us into new steps of obedience. How well I remember at college studying the book of Romans in my daily quiet time. I poured over the first nine chapters of that book for six months. I rewrote them in my own words. I memorized most of them. I took notes and wrote out questions and answers to each verse. The sovereignty of God and my response in grateful, holy obedience gripped me. I was not learning a system of doctrine and then imposing it on Scripture. I was following Scripture wherever it led and seeing how it all fit together in beautiful harmony. I was determined that my theology be shaped by all of Scripture—not just certain parts.

Long ago I had given up *words* like *luck, chance* and *accident*. But as I soaked myself in Scripture I saw that these non-Christian *concepts* had not been really uprooted. I would occasionally hitchhike home to suburban Baltimore from Dickinson College in Carlisle, Pennsylvania. Once I was boasting to a friend about God's goodness in supplying timely rides so that I arrived home in record speed. It was seventy miles over back roads, and one person went out of his way to take me to my doorstep. It occurred to me that if God was truly in control of these rides, perhaps he wanted me to do more than sit in silence or talk about the weather. I cringed inside, but I couldn't escape this conclusion.

I began to think about how I could find out if these drivers were interested in Christ without forcing myself on them. So began a series of car rides back and forth during which I prayed and then opened my mouth about my beliefs. I bought large quantities of a well-written pamphlet that I would leave with the driver in exchange for his kindness to me. Time seemed so short on those trips for I saw God use me. I learned how to live out my belief in a sovereign God.

In addition to our having a variety of relationships, we meet many different *types* of people. Various attempts have been made to categorize people needing to be evangelized.[1] Putting people into categories is dangerous if the result is to exclude certain types from evangelism or depersonalize someone. Yet, to be able to uncover root attitudes a person holds in common with other unbelievers, and to be able to develop questions and answers accordingly is a great aid in presenting the gospel. Because people are basically unchanged, we can even use descriptions of types of people made by Charles Bridges in 1849 to help us begin our categories:[2]

1. *The Ignorant and Indifferent.* This is the largest class of unbelievers. They need to be surprised and challenged to see their folly in throwing away their souls. We can tell them they are like people living in houses without fire insurance. Appropriate passages to present from Scripture would be the parable of the rich fool (Lk. 12:13-21) and the woman at the well (Jn. 4). We cannot be only gentle with the indifferent. Such people must be confronted and warned. They are to measure themselves by God's law. If their ignorance is real and not feigned, perhaps we can in meekness patiently instruct them—all the while prodding their conscience.

2. *The Self-righteous.* There are two types of self-righteous personalities: the non-religious who despise the idea of sin and the nominally religious whose hearts are like stone and, like the Pharisees, must be broken. Such people must be charged with

their self-righteousness (Mt. 5:20; Lk. 18:9), shown the difference between external righteousness and sins of the heart (Mt. 23:25), and helped to understand that their supposed righteousness is only relative (Lk. 18:9-14). We must hold a mirror up to these people to give them a glimpse of their pride.

3. *The False Christians.* These people may think they are Christians, but they are not. They need to be shown the nature of regeneration and the evidences of saving faith in 1 John. (Also Jn. 6:60-66; Lk. 14:25-33.)

4. *The Deliberate Atheists.* The vaunted intellectual problems they express are often moral problems of the heart (Jn. 3:14-20). If they do have real questions, however, these must be dealt with honestly and thoroughly. Jesus invites the skeptic, as he did Thomas, to examine more closely. "Honest answers to honest questions" should be our motto.

5. *The Seekers.* The last group consists of those who have awakened to their need for spiritual solutions. They possess some conviction of sin and guilt. We point them to Christ and his promises and continue to speak to their conscience. Get them to read passages of Scripture such as Isaiah 53, Psalm 51 and John 3.

Perhaps in our day we should add the category of cultists. You are likely to find in cults theological deviations from orthodoxy such as a false or inadequate basis of salvation and a false basis of authority. Many cults also use unbiblical modes of conducting themselves especially in their techniques of acquiring and training converts. These include among others: (1) isolation or involvement of the recruit so that the group controls all incoming information; (2) economic exploitation of recruits or an enslaving organizational structure; (3) esotericism, a deliberately created gap between the truth about the cult as given to the inner circle and a misleading image that is projected to others in the cult and to the public at large.[3]

Undoubtedly we will meet many members of cults, since they are very actively selling their point of view. The governing motif of the cults is a concern for power. We respond by affirming God's total power. The Eastern religions are on a quest for enlightenment, for they believe that the basic human problem is ignorance. We respond that sin is the basic problem and salvation is in Christ. Other cults stress community relationships and membership in a new family. We respond with a demonstration of Spirit-created fellowship in the body of Christ.

Many times we must be willing to confront and turn away these people because of their distorted teaching (2 Jn. 7-11; 2 Pet. 2). If we can gain a hearing with them, however, we need to keep these points in mind: Be brief and to the point; these people can take up our time unnecessarily by arguing. Be firm and identify ourselves as Bible-believing Christians; they may want to end the conversation right there. Be sure to emphasize grace, as this is a great distinction between our faith and theirs. Every cult member is ultimately relying on his or her own efforts for salvation. Be concerned and share personal experiences of free forgiveness, inner peace and joy found in the love of Jesus. Be careful to not spend too much time alone with cult members; have a mature Christian along. Be ready to give them some literature.

Getting Started
Any journey has to begin with the first step. Many of us never witness because we never start. We never open our mouths. We don't take the initiative. We are not aggressive enough in bringing Christ into the conversation. Perhaps we worry about what others will think of us. This is pride. Remember we can make others nervous because we are nervous. We are also often negative in our tone, adopting an Elmer Blurb approach, "You wouldn't be interested in God, would you? You're not? (Phew.) I didn't think so." (For questions non-Christians ask, see worksheet 9.)

If you are a gifted conversationalist, you may not have this problem of getting started on sharing the gospel. Of course, you will need to be careful not to rely only on your gifts instead of on the Lord. Most of us cringe inwardly and fumble in our attempts to convey the gospel, yet we should trust God and speak. The only thing we have to lose is our pride! Keep in mind some comments and questions that are natural and will help introduce your subject. We can think through beforehand what we are going to say or ask.

Figure A diagrams three conversations. The circles represent the layers of a person. The arrow shows different ways of conversing with him or her.

Most of us tend to talk only about safe, neutral, common things —the weather, food, prices and so on. We talk in the outside layer of our lives.

Perhaps a few go right to the heart of a person—their most personal thoughts—with almost no introduction. They ask, "Are you saved?" Many well-meaning people have used a bludgeon-type, hit-and-run approach to evangelism. By the grace of God, in spite of the method used, one in a thousand has come to the Savior. However, we often overlook the nine hundred and ninety-nine who are infinitely harder to reach because of this abrasive and blunt approach; and we fail to see that it is in spite of, rather than because of, the method used that the one person has come to know the Lord.[4] How often have you heard someone justify a large outlay of time and money in some evangelistic endeavor by saying, "Well, it was all worth it if one person came to the Lord." Was it? Maybe ten people would have come to the Lord if another approach had been used, and many more softened rather than turned away. We must learn to become aggressive without being obnoxious.

A better conversation model is to begin with common interests and seek to move deeper into values, attitudes and beliefs. We move gradually, yet directly, and with a purpose in mind. Our goal is to touch the conscience. One of the best ways to do this is by developing the art of questioning.

Some questions are better than others. God's answer will seem irrelevant if we ask questions like, "How may a person get fulfillment and purpose?" or, "What about your joy and happiness?" To such man-centered questions, our theological answers that

Figure A/Three Ways to Converse about Christ

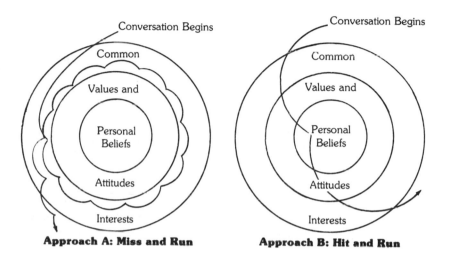

Approach A: Miss and Run

Approach B: Hit and Run

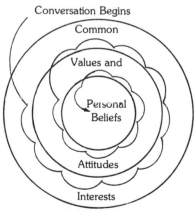

Approach C: Raise Questions and Make a Point

emphasize doctrines like justification will seem involved, academic and depressing. Evangelism is asking the right questions. It is leading them from secondary or misguided queries to the primary issues. We must meet and speak to people where they are, *and* we must know the gospel thoroughly—especially the focal point of justification by Christ through faith alone. The test of our evangelistic method is a simple question: does it make justification clear? The vital question is for a person to know whether or not he is acquitted by God.[5]

Conversation Turners

Enough for overall principles—here are examples of initiating sentences that might form a bridge into conversation about deeper issues. Some of these may seem awkward at first, nevertheless, we can prepare our own comments beforehand for many recurring circumstances. We don't need to pray for more opportunities, we just need to be ready to take advantage of the ones already there. Think of common situations you face, and develop your own response. (See Table 3.) The point of your remark is to help you find out if the Spirit is leading you to present more gospel content. Poor questions are ones that can be answered yes or no and don't lead into discussion. A good *response* leaves room for reaction and is open-ended. (See worksheets 4 and 5.)

In addition to conversation turners, there are also some general questions that open people up.[7] Perhaps you've been talking with someone for a while. Why not attempt to move into more important things? Here are some questions I like:

"What is your religious background?"

"How have your ideas about God changed since . . . (coming to college, getting married, having children, being in this job, the death of your friend, traveling overseas, reading that book, being in the military)?

Paul Little, an evangelist with Inter-Varsity for many years, suggested this progression:

"By the way, are you interested in spiritual things?" . . .

Table 3/Turning Conversations to Christ

Situation:	Someone complains about developments in the world or among certain people.
Response:	"Why do you think people do such terrible things? What do you think God thinks of that?"
Situation:	Someone you have helped thanks you.
Response:	"You're welcome. I want to help people. My perspective on life was really changed awhile back."
Situation:	Someone helps you.
Response:	"I really appreciate your help. What made you that way? . . . I feel God has called me to take a personal interest in people."
Situation:	You receive a compliment for something you've done.
Response:	"Why, thank you. I've gotten a new perspective on this since Jesus came into my life. I appreciate the world around me more—knowing who made it." (It is not improper just to say, "Thank you." It was you who did it. God uses you. Don't fall into an attitude of sickening self-abasement.)
Situation:	Someone asks you what you do.
Response:	(Scientist) "I'm involved in figuring out the structure of God's universe." (Give a descriptive or functional answer rather than where you work.)
Situation:	A comment is made on the difficulty of raising children.
Response:	"We're facing problems too. But we're encouraged by an interesting method that's quite helpful. We call it 'discipline with love,' and it's based on the Bible. Have you heard about it?"
Situation:	Someone is telling of their good fortune or luck in a matter.
Response:	"Do you think God has a reason for allowing you to experience this good thing? How do you account for the good things that have happened to you?"
Situation:	You're given too much change after a purchase.
Response:	"You know, at one time I would have kept the money, but Jesus Christ has turned my life around. Do you know Christ?"

"What do you think a real Christian is?" . . .

"Have you ever personally trusted Christ, or are you still on the way?" . . .

"How far on the way are you?" or, "Would you like to become a real Christian?" . . .[6]

James Kennedy, pastor of a large church in Florida, says these two questions have pinpointed basic issues for many:

"Have you come to a place in your spiritual life where you know for certain that if you were to die today you would go to heaven?"

"Suppose that you were to die tonight and stand before God, and he were to say to you, 'Why should I let you into my heaven?' What would you say?"[7]

Sure, these questions may seem a little awkward and forced at times. But how else are we going to find out what the Holy Spirit is doing in someone's life, especially those we will know only on a short-term basis? I've been amazed at how many people are genuinely interested in spiritual things. In visiting some students at random at the University of Delaware, many have thanked us for raising spiritual questions by saying, "You know I wasn't aware there were people who could help me with my questions. Since most people don't talk about religion seriously, I thought I was alone in my search. Thanks for coming by."

Conversation with a Direction

Many committed Christians flounder in personal evangelism because sharing religious ideas in conversation seems unnatural or forced. In many cases this problem exists because of a compartmentalization in their thinking—a thought-world divided into compartments labeled "gospel," "art," "marriage" and so on. The contents of any one of these compartments is only superficially related to the contents of another. As a result, the gospel seems an intruder in a conversation instead of being an integral part of a dynamic, ongoing dialog that encompasses the whole of life.

The solution to the problem is to eliminate the walls dividing the compartments and to relate religious ideas to ideas about art and marriage and other areas of everyday conversation. In other words, the solution is a unified, comprehensive thought-life. Christians who have such a thought-life can introduce religious ideas more naturally into a conversation. In a dialog they can move more easily from the non-Christian's immediate interests to more abstract levels of thought and from there to issues of a theological nature. For example:

Non-Christian Well, I've finally decided. I'm going to major in art.

Christian Great. What made you finally decide on that?

NC Well, I feel it's the best way to fulfill myself and to bring more beauty into the world.

C That's interesting. Why do you suppose you have this desire to make beautiful things?

NC That's hard to answer; but I know how much I enjoy the feeling I have when I make something new and beautiful.

C Yeah, I feel that way sometimes. I'm sure that's why I write poetry. Do you ever wonder if this striving to make beautiful things *means* anything? I mean that it might be an indication of some higher reality beyond the physical world?

NC You mean like a God? I think about that sometimes, but I just don't know. I think somebody must have designed the beauty in nature.

C That sure makes more sense than thinking everything is here by chance. You know, God didn't make much of a difference in my life until I understood he is a Creator who. . . .

The basic beliefs behind the Christian's questions includes these: (1) God is infinitely creative. (2) God is the source of beauty. (3) God created people in his image; therefore, we share God's creativity and yearn for beauty. These beliefs explain for the Christian why people strive to create beautiful things. So if the Christian can make the non-Christian consider the abstract question "Why do people strive to create beautiful things?" he or she can lead the unbeliever to consider Christian beliefs about the nature of God and the nature of man.

Some non-Christians will immediately be able to discuss abstract questions; most will not. If we can begin with questions about the non-Christian's experience, we can help the person begin thinking about more abstract (less immediate) questions, and then about theological ones. In discussing theological truths, we can keep the discussion from becoming abstract by showing in our own lives how this truth is applied. Then we can attempt to speak to the non-Christian's conscience as to how he or she should be applying (following through with) these truths. So, in Figure B, the movement of the dialog is from the outer circle to the center. This is a specific example of how Approach C in Figure A might work.[8]

Figure B/Conversational Evangelism

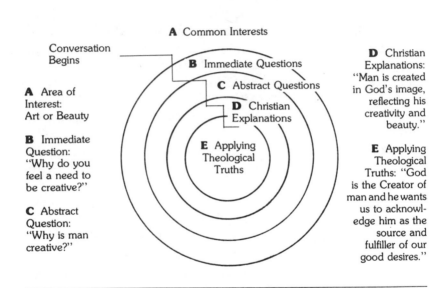

Conversation Begins

A Common Interests

A Area of Interest: Art or Beauty

B Immediate Question: "Why do you feel a need to be creative?"

C Abstract Question: "Why is man creative?"

B Immediate Questions

C Abstract Questions

D Christian Explanations

E Applying Theological Truths

D Christian Explanations: "Man is created in God's image, reflecting his creativity and beauty."

E Applying Theological Truths: "God is the Creator of man and he wants us to acknowledge him as the source and fulfiller of our good desires."

Once again we see that witnessing begins with merely being friendly and taking a genuine interest in the concerns of others. Christians who see life as a whole, not as separate unrelated parts, begin to be free to enjoy and explore all aspects of God's world. These interests lead naturally to a discussion of meaning, values and God.

What about Surveys?

Surveys are a common evangelistic technique, but I think the way most evangelicals use them is improper. Often Christians give people the impression that they are studying something, and the survey's answers will be tabulated, when, in fact, the survey is a tool designed to engage people in conversation. It seems much more honest to forget the survey itself and simply approach people on a personal level, such as: "Hello, I'm (your neighbor, fellow student, visiting for my church), and *I'm* interested in helping people with spiritual needs." You may have to add quickly, "We're not collecting money or interested in church membership," especially if the area you are visiting has been hit heavily by door-to-door religious sales reps.

The caller could then ask, "Do you have a few minutes to answer some questions?" Or, he or she could just go right into a question like the ones mentioned earlier. If the interviewee is responsive, the Christian could ask for more time to talk, having said at the outset the questions would only take a few minutes. One good follow-up is, "I'm interested in what you have said. I used to think that way too. One thing that helped me was to get an overview of what Jesus taught. Could we take fifteen minutes more? I'm sure you'd find it helpful." Here is a way to be direct, yet respectful and honest with people.

One type of survey that I think is justified is the one that attempts to discover those people whom the Holy Spirit has prepared by causing them to admit they have spiritual needs. Asking is the simplest way to find out if a person is willing to admit that some of his or her needs are spiritual. I have developed a spiritual needs survey that could be used to find people who are open (Table 4). The questions do not appeal to people's desires or attempt to manipulate them. By these questions we are asking, "Are you in any way interested in or aware that your needs are spiritual and there is a solution for such?" Their interest possibly indicates that they are seekers who have been awakened by God to their true needs.

I do not hand the survey to the person being questioned, but merely use it as a prompter for the person learning to witness. After a while, Christians can dispense with the sheet and personalize the interview even more. I often begin by saying, "Wherever I go, I'm interested in meeting people. I especially like to find out if they have any sense of spiritual needs. I'd be interested in your response to eight questions that I've asked others. Are you interested in hearing them?"

If a person says they are interested in hearing a summary of the main theme of the Bible, I explain it will take about fifteen minutes and ask if we could sit down. I give them their own copy of my gospel outline and ask them to follow along. (In a later

---

Table 4/Spiritual Interest Questionnaire

"We're asking people for five minutes to answer several brief questions. Can you give us five minutes?

"We're interested in personally becoming acquainted with those who have spiritual concerns, so these questions concern your spiritual interest and background."

---

1. What is your religious background or upbringing?

---

2. Are you now experiencing any meaning in your religion?

---

3. Can you give one example of how your religion affects your behavior; that is, how it makes a practical difference in your life?

---

4. When it comes to spiritual matters would you describe yourself as unconcerned or interested?

---

5. Do you think of yourself as a person created by God and therefore accountable to him for the way you live?

---

6. Do you ever think of yourself as in need of God's forgiveness for things you've thought, said, or done?

---

7. In your opinion, who is Jesus Christ?

---

8. Summarize in one sentence what you think is the main theme of the Bible.

Unconcerned: "Thank you for your time. Perhaps as you reflect upon these questions you might come to realize the Bible has a lot of practical help and meaning for our lives. Thanks."

Concerned: "Thank you for your time. Your answers seem to indicate an interest in spiritual matters, and especially your response to the question about _____ . Could we take a few more minutes to talk? . . ."

"Many people have found it helpful to hear a brief outline summary of the main theme of the Bible. Could I do this for you now?"

section in this chapter I discuss further the proper way to use an outline of the gospel.) If they answer no I thank them and offer free literature they can read when convenient. Sometimes you will not use this question but say, "Your answer to question _____ interested me. I'd like to know more about why you think that way if you have time." A natural conversation about the gospel often follows.

The Uninterested

What do we do if people just are not interested? We let them go their way, as Jesus did the moral young man (Lk. 18:18-29). We should not feel guilty or embarrassed, even though we are disappointed. We do not fail when we recognize and follow the Holy Spirit's leading. That young man would not bow to Christ's lordship. Jesus loved him and bore the pain of rejection. So must we.

Some man-centered evangelists, upon hearing the young man ask about eternal life, would have been sure not to let him escape. After getting him to pray to receive Christ, they would likely ask him to give his testimony within the week. When his spiritual interest declined, he would be regarded as carnal, and earnest Christians would urge another level of Christian duty or a special experience on him. Such people are swept into a Christian group before the Spirit finishes his regenerative work. Thinking they are Christians, these "converts" move within the Christian community motivated by purely natural desires and remain parked immovably on the pew.

God's timing is always best. This was indelibly impressed upon me when I participated in a husband-coached childbirth clinic. We were expecting our first child and I was anxious to help Suzanne in whatever way I could. Every Tuesday night we met with other eager parents under the leadership of a trained nurse. We learned what would happen in those last hours just before delivery. We memorized and practiced our teamwork for the big moment. But what brought on the dropping, turning, and final expulsion of the baby? The nurse said, "There isn't anything you can do to determine the moment of birth. When that baby's ready, nothing is going to stop him.'' God takes over, and the timing is all in his hands. That's also true in the timetable for the new birth.

Which is better, to push someone hastily into the kingdom of God and give him a false basis for his supposed salvation, or to speak the truth and let him go until God's good timing is right? We will have both liberty and joy when our witnessing is controlled by faith in God's sovereignty.

We can picture ourselves as fishermen who throw out the net as often and as wide as possible. Our net is made up of questions and statements about the gospel. As the net entangles a fish (as a person shows an interest in spiritual things), we have an indication that God's Spirit has gone before us creating interest. We may find that even those who are at first hostile are really being worked on by the Spirit but they struggle against him—often because they have a conscience that bothers them. A good question to ask is, "What has caused you to feel so negative about Christianity?" Then get ready to listen and learn.

Most people are not hostile; rather, they are indifferent. They seem happy and content. Does the gospel have anything to say to these people? Must they admit failure before we can relate Christ to them? No. Christ is the source of all our strength and happiness too. The seed idea to plant is, "God is to be thanked for his goodness to you, and the purpose of his goodness is to bring you to repentance" (see Rom. 2:4). It is vital that we present God as holy and the law as absolute. People are never as indifferent as they seem. We need to discover what they are concerned about and then move from this concern to the deepest issues of life.

I would say something like this: "You know there were people with just your attitude in Jesus' day. Did you know the Bible describes exactly your indifference and the consequences of it? Jesus himself dealt with this attitude on several occasions. Jesus said, 'It is not the healthy who need a doctor, but the sick. I have not come to call the righteous, but sinners to repentance' (Lk. 5:31-32). Jesus did not come to help those who thought they were well;

he would help those who knew they were not well. Jesus admitted that some people thought they had no need of him. 'Thanks, but no thanks,' they said. 'I can do perfectly well by myself (with perhaps a little help from my friends),' was their ingrained attitude. To these people Jesus had nothing to say. If a person has no needs (the sickness of sin), then he or she doesn't need a Savior. In this sense Jesus did not come for all—he came only for sinners. You assume you can heal (save) yourself. As long as you do not admit your needs (either because you are blind to them or you are too proud) you are part of those people who in age after age have rejected Jesus as Savior and Lord. Yes, rejected. You can't be neutral in the presence of a physician who has come to tell you heart surgery is needed. Your rejection of Christ becomes a fact. It is as clear as if you wrote today's date on a card and the sentence, 'I have this day rejected Jesus Christ as my Savior and Lord,' and signed it.''

Persistent indifference to Jesus and his claims is an evidence of the completeness of Satan's bondage. Why? Because Satan's most effective work is done when he deceives people into thinking all is well. It is far more effective to lull people to sleep in indifference (they can even take pride in their self-sufficiency and open-mindedness), than to have them adopt an openly hostile attitude toward Christ. Their hostility might cause them to wonder at some point why they are so upset about the whole thing. Satan could lose them for they are awake and fighting! The sleep of complacency is much more effective.

I've met young men who have reacted to a friend's engagement with, "I'll never get married. Look at that fool! He's really caught now!" No matter how wonderful you tell them that love is, it makes no impression. Of course, the reason they see this exclusive lifetime commitment of marriage as frightful and limiting is just this: they aren't in love yet! They haven't been pierced by someone's love for them. They haven't admitted their need for such a love and begun to reach out by returning love. Of course they aren't ready to give themselves away to obtain another! Marriage (and religion) is conceived as a crutch for the weak. Our culture brainwashes us into thinking that independence—do it on your own—is maturity and strength. Dependence—admission of weakness, failure, needs, others—is almost anti-American. Of course, this is sheer pride.

In conclusion, there is very little that can be said to the self-complacent. We can pray for God to humble them. He does this in either of two ways: he woos us in our blessings and warns us in our tragedies. We can continue to hope that the constancy of our care for the indifferent unbelievers will prick their consciences.

One woman in my church, hearing that I was writing a book on evangelism and thinking that therefore I must be an expert on the topic, built up all her courage to ask me this burning question: "I was told that people were just waiting to hear the gospel and believe. You know, I've been trying for years to find all these people who are eagerly awaiting my gospel presentation. Can you tell me where they are?" She, along with many, had become discouraged. When she was told that "the fields were white for harvest," she thought the grain would fall off easily with each evangelistic conversation. But is that what the Lord means when he speaks of the ripe fields?

Reasoning with People

Apologetics (the defense of the faith) has much value in witnessing and can be an effective tool to prepare the way for the gospel. All reality testifies to a Creator (Ps. 19; Rom. 1:20). The validity of Christianity is confirmed through archaeology, history and various sciences—but these are not proofs. For even if we are able to prove from archaeology that Christ died, we are still not able to scientifically prove it was for our sins. Thus, rational evidences are only of limited value.

The most effective apologetic is to admit our presuppositions[9] and show how they make sense of both the real world and the creature who lives in it. We ask unbelievers—we prod them—to look at life through our glasses. We expose their own assumptions to them (for many have unconscious beliefs about the world) and ask them to evaluate how consistently they live out those assumptions. We show them the dead end and dehumanizing results of their positions. By reading some books on this topic we can get a feel for the trends in our culture and discern the non-Christian assumptions underlying them.[10] We each need to concentrate our study on one area of culture (such as art, science, philosophy or politics) and/or one trend (such as relativism or humanism). We need to learn how to lovingly take off the protective roof of a false world view that people have built over their heads to keep God away. We can challenge the idol-manufacturing mind of modern people.

If we love people, we will desire to understand what they are thinking. Our apologetics will not be just to cross swords with them, but to help. The sharpness of our reasoning can be an ornament to our witness. It can also be a blight—for the danger is to become proud or to extensively "pre-evangelize," that is, spend all our time preparing a person to hear the gospel. We then feel good about how articulate we are but never get to the point of explaining the work of Christ and urging our listeners to repent and believe. God's chosen instrument in conversion is his Word not our reasoning ability. So we must continue to study our culture but at the same time remember that books and films are only one means. We do not have to be intellectuals to analyze our culture. Not only can we talk things over with our family and Christian friends, but we can put ourselves in situations that are cross-cultural (international students, ghetto dwellers, visit other countries ourselves) and totally secular (university courses, many types of jobs) where we can learn firsthand.

Speaking to the Conscience

God has built into all of us a point of contact, a sense of the deity and a sense of responsibility for our moral actions (Rom. 2:14-15). This sense may be buried, denied or suppressed but it is there even in avowed atheists. The truth of the gospel fits with the way people are made. Our task is to remind them of what deep down they already know: God exists and has created them to act rightly. When I came to realize the implications of this truth for my personal witnessing, I was liberated almost as much as when I learned of God's sovereignty in salvation. I now saw how much I had going for me every time I transmitted God's message, for he had put a built-in receptor inside each person. We are to reinforce, educate and illuminate the conscience of unbelievers.[11]

As we touch the conscience, we bring truth alongside people's lives. Ultimately, the acceptance of the gospel is a moral problem, not an intellectual problem. When people tell me they are atheists, they are not just telling me about the way they think. They also tell me something about the way they live. Jesus accused people of not being willing to come to the light because of hatred in their hearts. The light of Christ exposes their evil deeds, and so they prefer darkness (Jn. 3:19-20) not because they have doubts, but because they love their sin and don't want to change. In showing people their moral guilt, we are not to leave them in despair nor tell them they are worthless. Hopefully, our witness will show them their guilt and need of forgiveness, not simply their despair and need for an answer. To elicit conviction (which is really a merciful work of the Holy Spirit) is not cruel, but kind. We can repent of guilt, but not of despair.

Conscience delivers messages (judgments) to us concerning whether an action or attitude of ours is right or wrong. It is like the thud of the judge's gavel in the courtroom of our conscience when the verdict of acquitted or guilty is rendered.

Some Christians have an *insensitive* conscience; others have an *oversensitive* conscience. The insensitive conscience leads to hardness of heart or "carnal carelessness" as the Puritans put it. Will Barker suggests two remedies.[12] The remedy for the hardened conscience is to use the law of God (all the commandments) to confront the old man in order to bring the person to renewed repentance.

The oversensitive conscience leads to despair, fear, lack of confidence. To remedy this we use the grace of God (all the promises) to assure the new man in Christ and to bring him to renewed faith. This principle regarding the conscience demonstrates that repentance and faith compose the base line of the Christian life, as well as being the means by which we first enter that life. To put it in theological terms, just as justification flows from repentance and faith, so likewise does sanctification.

Jesus spoke to the conscience of his hearers. He put his finger on a sensitive spot in the Samaritan woman's heart when he told her to go and call her husband. He shamed Nicodemus when he indicated that as a teacher he should know of spiritual matters. There must have been a sting in the conscience of the moral young man when Jesus told him to stop coveting.

Paul, too, spoke powerfully to the conscience. We find him concluding his testimony to King Agrippa (Acts 26) by saying that he knows the king believes the prophets and by praying that he might be converted. Paul emphasizes that all he did, he did openly (not in a corner). All of Paul's hearers knew the way he had lived before and after his conversion. He could look straight at the Sanhedrin (Acts 23:1) because his own conscience was clear (Acts 24:16)—commending him rather than condemning him. Paul witnessed before Felix about righteousness, self-control and the judgment to come (Acts 24:25—interesting content for evangelism) and his words struck fear in Felix's heart. In renouncing deception and distortion, Paul states his evangelistic goal: "setting forth the truth plainly we commend ourselves to every man's conscience in the sight of God. . . . Since, then, we know what it is to fear the Lord, we try to persuade men. What we are is plain to God, and I hope it is also plain to your conscience" (2 Cor. 4:2; 5:11).

We realize that only the Holy Spirit can sensitize the conscience and bring conviction, but the Spirit has given us tools in the Ten Commandments, the Sermon on the Mount and other passages that explain true righteousness. It is not that we merely quote these Scriptures to others, but that we incorporate their emphasis into our conversation as we delve into the values of people. As we talk with people, we can move from one area where they feel guilt into all other aspects of their lives, showing them that the Bible's diagnosis of their need is that they have a sinful nature. Here are some questions to use in appealing to the conscience after we have discussed the gospel. We need to be careful not to use these to manipulate people while remembering that the *loving* thing is to show others their guilt.

"Are there things in your life you are not willing to face and have God change?"

"Isn't the real issue that you can't face your sin and guilt before God?"

"If I were to answer all your questions about Christ satisfactorily, would you be willing to come to him? . . . Why not?"

"Assuming that God exists and has created you—don't you have a responsibility to him? Have you ever thanked him?"

"If you had recorded in a notebook all your thoughts and judgments of others for the last day, and then lost it, how would you feel?"

"How do you know what love is—and that you're not actually running away from it?"

In directing unbelievers in how to become Christians (closing with Christ as the old Puritans termed it), nothing can be more succinct, theologically accurate, and practical than the classic description given in *Pilgrim's Progress* by John Bunyan's character, Hopeful. Listen as Hopeful explains to Christian how he came to believe on the Lord Jesus Christ.[13]

Hopeful: He (Faithful) bade me go to Him, and see. Then I said, "It was presumption;" but he said, "No; for I was invited to come" (Matt. 11:28). Then he gave me a book of Jesus's inditing, to encourage me the more freely to come; and he said concerning that book, That every jot and tittle thereof stood firmer than heaven and earth (Matt. 24:35). Then I asked him, what I must do when I came; and he told me, I must entreat upon my knees, with all my heart and soul, the Father to reveal Him to me. Then I asked him further, "How I must make my supplication to Him?'' and he said, "Go, and thou shalt find Him upon a mercy-seat, where He sits all the year long to give pardon and forgiveness to them that come. I told him that I knew not what to say when I came; and he bid me say to this effect, "God be merciful to me a sinner, and make me to know and believe in Jesus Christ; for I see that if His righteousness had not been, or I have not faith in that righteousness, I am utterly cast away. Lord, I have heard that Thou art a merciful God, and hast ordained that Thy Son Jesus Christ should be the Saviour of the world: and moreover, that Thou art willing to bestow Him upon such a poor sinner as I am (and I am a sinner indeed); Lord, take therefore this opportunity, and magnify Thy grace in the salvation of my soul, through Thy Son Jesus Christ. Amen.''

Bunyan says that Christ did *not* at first reveal himself to Hopeful, but *only as he kept on praying.* In the midst of increasing conviction of sin he said,

"Lord, I am a great, a very great sinner;" and He answered, "My grace is sufficient for thee" (11 Cor. 12:9). Then I said, "But, Lord, what is believing?" And then I saw from that saying, "He that cometh to Me shall never hunger; and he that believeth on Me shall never thirst" (John 6:35), that believing and coming were one: and that he that came, that is, that ran out in his heart and affections after salvation by Christ, he indeed believed in Christ. . . . From all which I gathered, that I must look for righteousness in His person, and for satisfaction for my sins by His blood; that what He did in obedience, to his Father's law, and in submitting to the penalty thereof, was not for Himself, but for him that will accept it for his salvation, and be thankful. And now was my heart full of joy; mine eyes full of tears; and mine affections running over with love to the name, people, and ways of Jesus Christ.

Using an Outline

We have already seen that evangelism is teaching. In addition, we saw that although the entire Scripture points to Christ and salvation, there are central truths to emphasize in witnessing. Examining 1 Corinthians 15, the speeches in Acts, the shape of Mark's Gospel, and certain other passages in the New Testament, we can conclude that there was a fixed pattern in the evangelistic preaching of the early church. Of course the early evangelists were undoubtedly flexible and took into account the background and understanding of their listeners. The early Christians held a common belief, but their modes of expression depended on their own intellectual and spiritual backgrounds. The kerygma (the New Testament preaching) was variety-in-unity. When we read each of the four Gospels, we should ask, "In what circumstances and for what purpose was this story included?" We soon see that many of the incidents were recorded for their evangelistic impact. We should use them in the same way.[14]

Jesus' approach was constantly shaped not only by the truth he wished to convey, but by the background of the unbeliever. He treated individuals as unique.[15] His approaches to a Jewish Rabbi, Nicodemus (Jn. 3) and a Samaritan woman with many love affairs (Jn. 4) were different. Allowing this variety to stand, we can still see a definite table of contents to the gospel message.

In spite of the abuse to which a gospel outline can be subject, it is a very helpful tool. It is useful in training Christians about what constitutes the message, thus keeping them on the track when witnessing. A gospel summary is also helpful to a non-Christian who is often totally ignorant of what the Bible teaches. However, any outline that is used mechanically or used in a way that doesn't provide for listening, can be harmful. We are to listen, talk and question with a view to understanding a person's problem and applying the gospel at that point. (See appendix B, worksheet 8.)

After a conversation has turned to religion, I have found it quite natural to introduce the idea of a gospel summary in this way: "I think it would be helpful if I tried to give you the frame of reference behind a number of my statements. How about if I take fifteen minutes to give you an overview of the central theme of the Bible, sort of the big picture—what the Bible calls the good news? Then you can see what I'm trying to express and how the different statements I'm making fit together—O.K.?''

At this point, either from memory or by looking at the outline with the person, I use the four points of Table 2 to convey the content of the gospel. I might read a passage or verse from the Bible to substantiate each point, showing that the Bible, and not my own opinions, is the source of authority. If you choose to look at Scripture passages, thirty minutes might be a better time estimate.

Running through a summary of the gospel does not evangelize a person nor does the use of this tool guarantee your effectiveness, but it can help. For years, I reacted against any rote use of a method. I tried to be personal with others and let them lead the conversation where they wanted it to go. I would bring in Christian truth as I could. This is still a valid approach in some of our relationships. Later, however, I began where they were and kept bringing them back to one element of the gospel (such as the biblical view of God or the biblical definition of sin) in order to leave a message in their conscience. This approach also has its place and can result in a significant contribution to a person's understanding of the gospel. I did not always cover all the points in a gospel outline or follow their order. But I was sure to define and give synonyms for the Bible terms I used.

Many times, however, I have witnessed in a weak way simply because I have not stated clearly my main point—focusing on God as the Creator-Redeemer. The lack of a theistic framework in the minds of most people today makes a statement of our framework necessary for communication. Our ultimate confidence is in the power of God's Word—the naked gospel message.

Once we have taken an opportunity to present the gospel, we will want to conclude by asking questions such as these:

"What do you think of such a God who is a Creator and Redeemer?"

"Have you ever turned from relying on yourself and trusted in Christ?"

"At what point (truth) in my comments did you feel most uncomfortable?"

"Have you ever considered yourself a sinner according to the biblical definition?"

"What do you think of what Jesus has done for sinners?"

Perhaps after presenting an outline of the gospel someone may still say, "But even you Christians differ among yourselves in what you teach." Yes, this is true, for several reasons. First, the Bible allows us to hold differing opinions on certain issues. We have the freedom and liberty to apply the principles of Scripture to our own situation. Thus, some Christians treat Sunday as a day exclusively for worship while others include an emphasis on the family and enjoyment of God's creation. Some Christians totally abstain from fermented liquor and others drink in moderation. Second, Christians are still sinners, albeit forgiven sinners. We sometimes distort Scripture to fit our own preconceptions and our own desires. Third, there are at times a scarcity of good teachers (ministers or prophets) who can help us to understand the doctrine of the Bible and its application. Fourth, we sometimes lack depth in our personal Bible study.

Nevertheless, it is important to note that on most of the central truths of the Bible, true Christians have stood united. Part of the problem in a question like this is that many who have identified themselves with Christianity are simply using it to further their own ends. A definition of a Christian is necessary if you want to discuss differences among "Christians." This definition is found in Acts 11:26, "The disciples were first called Christians at Antioch." A good place to start is with a study of the book of Acts to see just what constituted a Christian—what did such a person believe and do? Inextricably bound up with his faith in Christ was a faith in God's Word. That Word is now our Bible, and we cannot separate Christ from the Scriptures. Although a true Christian does not worship the Bible, he does worship Christ as revealed in the Scriptures —and none other.

It is interesting to see that the creeds of the various churches that held to historic and biblical Christianity do agree on major doctrines. This solidarity is a tremendous testimony to the timelessness of the truths in the Bible and to the Bible's clarity in essential matters.

Some of the divisions among Christians are healthy. Their separation allows them to reach a particular culture or specific goals. Since organizational unity is secondary to the spiritual tasks we are trying to accomplish, we are not concerned to be all under one administrative umbrella. Where this variety has led to duplication, rivalry, wasted funds and a spirit of prideful independence it is wrong. We must admit our error. However, there can be strength in diversity. We eschew unity for unity's sake. Jesus advocated unity based on the oneness of thought, word and relationship similar to his unity with the Father (Jn. 17). True unity is based on being of one mind (substantial doctrinal agreement).

Most people we meet will not be prepared by the Holy Spirit to turn to Christ after only one interchange. We will therefore need to go back and work through the gospel at the point each person specifies as his or her hang-up. Deep truths seldom sink in all at once (although we should always be alert to exceptions). A person is not evangelized until the Spirit of God makes these truths real to the heart. We must continue to labor with these same truths until they stir the whole person to respond.

Walking alongside the Needy

The summer after my first year in college, I worked with my father in his tree-care business. This left my nights free. I wanted to use some of this time to share the joy of God's forgiveness with others. Through Inter-Varsity and a church near campus, I had grown tremendously in my faith during my freshman year and saw clearly that evangelism was not a spectator sport.

My first thought was of an inner-city mission in Baltimore I had heard about. One hot June evening I drove downtown to help at the evening service. I felt funny parking our new car right in front of the mission, so I left it down the street. When I walked up to the front door of the building, I found it was locked! I rattled it so much that a man came to investigate. He peered out at me through the screen and quickly sized me up. With a gruff voice and a wave of the hand he said, "The meeting has already started. You're late. Go around to the back door and they'll assign you a bed for the night." I soon realized that my mistaken identity as "one of them" could provide me with a golden opportunity for an insider's look at urban mission work. I declined the stub for a bed from the bedraggled helper in the basement and headed upstairs for the "gospel meeting."

The first fifteen rows were empty; I chose a seat in the back next to a rather restless fellow. When the meeting dismissed, I merged with the line as all the men dutifully shook hands with the speaker. Each was asked if he was a born-again Christian. Most said yes, including my new friend. (He later told me that this answer was the easiest way to avoid a hassle.) Once I got through this line unrecognized, I asked my friend what there was to do now—for it was only eight o'clock. Remarking on his hunger, he said he was headed for the streets. A mission helper reminded him this would mean the loss of his bed since none was allowed on the street again after the meeting for fear he would bring liquor back inside. I asked if I could join him.

For the next five hours, I walked the dark city streets with a man whom I had never seen before and who was completely different from me. He never asked me about myself, rather he accepted me as a fellow traveler and told me all I wanted to know about his sordid background. When we parted late that night, I felt compelled to reveal my own identity. I tried to draw a crude comparison between Christ's coming to walk alongside the needy and my conviction that God had sent me that night to accompany him. He was stunned, and I was able to open the gospel plainly to him, but with no apparent response. I left him some literature with my name and phone number and a small amount of money.

I learned a lot that night. I saw that people like my friend required someone living with them and being available. A nightly foray would not do. Then I realized my hypocrisy in driving across town to help others when I had never reached out to those in my own suburban neighborhood. Fear and depression seized me. My conscience nagged me.

Reluctantly I came to a conclusion. I was to start where God had placed me! My home and my neighborhood was my Jerusalem that summer. I was young and inexperienced. I had never done house-to-house visitation before. I had no idea what to do. How I began to dread Tuesday nights—the time I had set aside to walk those long streets of our community. I clearly remember wishing for a rainstorm! Ours was a small community in which people settled for a good chunk of their lives. Our family was well known and had lived there for thirty years. I found it hardest to go to the doors of people I had known longest.

Gradually I learned to express myself. I was alone, afraid, yet joyful by the end of each evening. I could honestly say I didn't want their money or church membership. I introduced myself as a neighbor and asked for a few minutes of their time. I learned that I needed to help them understand what was expected of them. So, by the third week, I made my request more specific. I asked if I could take five minutes to read a passage from the New Testament (Acts 17:22-34) or the Old Testament (Is. 53), since some were Jewish. If the answer was yes, I read the passage aloud. I explained I was doing this because I wanted others to consider Jesus, the God-man who had changed my life. Keeping to my time limit, I ended by asking, "Do you have any questions or comments?" Many did. I always left an appropriate pamphlet or a New Testament.

The experience of joy in witnessing has led me into a lifetime of sharing the gospel, sometimes with close friends and relatives, sometimes with strangers in faraway places—the boardwalk in Ocean City, Maryland; the beaches of Ft. Lauderdale, Florida; New York's Central Park, Greenwich Village, Washington Square. I've been in prisons, migrant camps and in swank resorts like Michigan's Mackinac Island and Colorado's town parks. I've seen people listen with intensity in Europe and South Africa.

God leads Christians as they act. Nothing can substitute for *doing*. Too long have we followed a rationalist model rather than an apprenticeship model in evangelism. We can get together with a Christian friend, pray together and study the content of the gospel. Then with some good literature we can go out together for one or two hours, door to door or to a place where people congregate. I think I know all the objections coming to your mind—I've used every one. But I know none of them hold water. The only thing we can lose is our pride—and that might be a good thing for all of us!

Some have made a fetish of this kind of witnessing, calling it "cold turkey," "contact" or "one-on-one" evangelism. I prefer the name "personal witnessing," for it is possible to treat strangers as individuals and not be mechanical or impersonal. The value of sharing as much of the gospel as we can with as many people as we can is not measured in numbers of converts. I have not been privileged to be the last link in the chain of witness to very many people. The value is in knowing that we have obeyed our Lord and have been a reinforcer of his truths to many consciences. The value can be seen in how your experiences of witnessing change your Christian life. The value is in becoming an initiator of conversations about Christ with friends and family too.

What happened to me as I began witnessing? God quickened and deepened a conviction of the sovereignty of God, a joy that God uses me, a confidence that his Word is true, a desire to forsake my own sins and lead a holy life, a hunger to study the Bible, a fervency in prayer, a concern and love for others.

The point is not to depend on a program of evangelism that becomes a narrow tradition (every Monday at 7 P.M. we do our witnessing for the week.) Our aim is to use these methods to develop *an evangelistic way of life.* As I have continued to share the gospel, I am now more aware of people around me (especially strangers). I am more friendly, listen more carefully, ask more leading questions, give away more literature. I am more bold with close friends and relatives, taking advantage of our long-term relationship to help them understand the various points of the gospel, to show the difference Christ makes in my life and to stir their consciences over a period of time.

I don't care what you call it, but if your church or organization does not provide some means whereby Christians can go out together and witness, it is failing in God's calling to train evangelists. (See worksheets 10, 11 and 12.)

We can learn to expect and hope in God not ourselves. As we put ourselves in situations we cannot handle, we can watch God work! One reason God may not be real to us anymore is because we are no longer desperate. If the Holy Spirit were taken out of our lives today, what would change? What are we now depending on God to do for us that we could not carry on pretty well in our own strength?

Our Goal—Disciples

To evangelize is for whole people to present the whole gospel to the whole person.

Our goal is not just decisions, but disciples and a faithful witness that glorifies God. We do all we can to avoid premature birth and deformed children, trusting God to bring his "full-term" children into the kingdom. To clarify the difference between decisioning and discipling, in Table 5 I have set up a series of contrasts between two evangelistic methodologies that have different goals and therefore conflict in approaches to witnessing.

Once again, in Table 5 we see how imperative right theology is to our evangelistic methodology. Is this being overly precise? No. As one of the Puritans said when rebuked for his conscientiousness, "Sir, I serve a precise God!" And, as one who follows in the good points of our Puritan heritage, J. I. Packer puts it this way:

Evangelism and theology for the most part go separate ways, and the result is great loss for both. When theology is not held on course by the demands of evangelistic communication, it grows abstract and speculative, wayward in method, theoretical

Table 5/The Goal in Witnessing Affects the Methods

Man-centered	God-centered
Goal—decisions, mental assent, immediate responses by praying.	*Goal—disciples, conversion of the whole person, isolation so they will call on God for mercy.*
Get them to agree with certain facts or laws.	Responsibly teach the gospel clearly, forcefully, extensively.
Work through a simple step-by-step method, thus "evangelizing."	Communicate the truths of the gospel repetitively, patiently.
Show as many advantages as possible.	Balance the benefits of the gospel with the sacrificial demands of the gospel.
Get them to pray with you.	Allow time for prayer in their own words—preferably alone.
Trigger their residual powers for freely choosing God.	Face them with the impossibility of saving themselves or exercising faith on their own.
Use an outward physical sign to confirm spiritual reality—signing a card, raising a hand, going forward, repeating a prayer.	Emphasize baptism, partaking of the Lord's Supper to proclaim his death, changing sinful ways of life.
Challenge their will with adventure, entice their emotions with excitement.	Present truth to the mind, call on will to obey, expect the emotions to follow.
Give immediate assurance—don't allow them to doubt their own sincerity.	Let the Holy Spirit give assurance via subjective inner witness and objective biblical evidence of changed life.

in interest and irresponsible in stance. When evangelism is not fertilized, fed and controlled by theology, it becomes a stylized performance seeking its effect through manipulative skills rather than the power of vision and the force of truth. Both theology and evangelism are then, in one important sense, *unreal,* false to their own God-given nature; for all true theology has an evangelistic thrust, and all true evangelism is theology in action.[16]

In discipleship evangelism, a non-Christian is pointed to Jesus Christ as Savior and Lord. We do not hide the demands of discipleship behind the benefits of salvation. Unbelievers will not, at the point of conversion, understand all the implications of Christ's lordship. Learning to be an obedient disciple develops through successive crisis experiences that call for repentance and faith throughout the Christian life. Nevertheless, we cannot divide Christ by presenting him as Savior and not as Lord.

The Lausanne Covenant, agreed on by evangelical leaders from over one hundred and fifty different nations, says: "The results of evangelism include obedience to Christ, incorporation into his church and responsible service in the world."[17] Let's examine each of these in turn.

First, if our response to the gospel is authentic, it will issue in sincere (not perfect) obedience. A true sheep hears and follows the good shepherd (Jn. 10:4). We can evaluate a profession of faith by its fruits. "When God prompts faith, He prompts it in such a way that the believer becomes hungry for Scripture. He wants to live by every word which proceeds from the mouth of God. He desires the pure spiritual milk."[18]

Second, an authentic conversion will lead to a love for the brethren (1 Jn. 3:14-15). A Christian who desires to be a loner is inconceivable in terms of the New Testament. We have been placed in a body and must identify ourselves with the new humanity. We become part of a community of believers and can work out our new adherence to truth and love in our relationships with others.

Paradoxically, the Christian turns both *from* the world and *to* the world. He turns *from* its lifestyle *to* its life need. He turns from irresponsible sin to responsible service. . . . The evangelist, on the way from Jerusalem to his city-wide crusade in Jericho, will not, in passing, toss a tract or decision card to the man who has fallen among thieves, but will stop to minister and care for him. Any professed conversion that doesn't issue in new obedience is spurious. True conversion turns a person from a rebel to a servant. Our Lord evangelized by demanding subjection to Himself. A Christian is a person under authority.[19]

Obedience and holiness are not optional. Paul exhorts people to "prove their repentance by their deeds" (Acts 26:18-23). He is not teaching works as qualifications for salvation—but as evidence of genuine repentance. Faith alone saves; but that faith that is alone (unaccompanied by good works) is not saving faith. Thus, service is the third evidence of true conversion.

If discipleship is our goal in God-centered evangelism, what do we need to witness? We need a knowledge of others and a knowledge of Scripture.

We need to know how people think, rationalize, hurt, hope and desire. We must know how and where they live. We must constantly forward the gospel to a new address because the recipient is repeatedly changing residence.[20] Our goal is to tie into, complement and reinforce with truth the work the Holy Spirit has already begun in the consciences of those we meet. To reach that goal, we need to spend time with people, all sorts of people. We should read and travel as we have opportunity. We all can become more self-conscious. We can learn a lot about the way people operate by being more aware of how we ourselves operate. Any occasion is one in which we can show our interest in others. Be a friend, a listener, an observer, a questioner, a lover, a proclaimer!

Lloyd-Jones, sums up our goal in knowing the Bible this way: If you want to be able to present the Gospel and the truth in the only right and true way, you must be constant students of the Word of God; you must read it without ceasing. . . . You must read what I call Biblical theology, the explanation of the great doctrines of the New Testament, so that you may come to understand them more and more clearly. . . . The work of this ministry does not consist merely in giving our own personal experience or talking about our own lives, or the lives of others—but in presenting the truth of God in as simple and clear a manner as possible. . . . We must make time to equip ourselves for the task, realizing the serious and terrible responsibility of the work.[21]

In the words of the Great Commission (Mt. 28:19-20), we are to "go"—not just talk but act; "make disciples"—not just professors of faith but possessors of the Son; "baptizing"—not just leaving them on their own but incorporating them into a biblical church; "teaching"—not just offering a few slickly packaged gospel facts but everything in Christ's commandments. Our goal is a practical con-formity to the Word of God. (See worksheet 7.)

I think of how one student responded to God-centered evangelism. She was part of a team of Christian students working at a large amusement park on the East Coast. These students had been asked to work at this park for a ten-week period during the summer. There they would have what I hoped would be a natural and life-changing influence on the other employees. During their off hours we began to build a caring Christian community. We also learned to see God as the Lord of our evangelism. We poured over Scripture passages discussing God's role in salvation and our privilege to be his ambassadors. We repented of our shallow views of God, trust in techniques and fear of others. This opened the door in a new way for this girl to witness. In her words, "When I came, I thought you were going to force me to witness. All you did was open the Bible and give us a big view of God as sovereign. Now that I see him, I *want* to witness. I feel freed and confident."

A gospel that elevates man and dethrones God is not the gospel. In God-centered evangelism, there is a return to the royal gospel which exalts God's grace at every point. The patient teaching of the doctrines of the gospel in a balanced and full way is greatly needed in our day. Do you want a snapshot of an evangelist in action? Then look at Ezekiel preaching in a cemetary to dry bones and commanding them to come alive (Ezek. 37:1-10), or watch Jesus as he stands at the tomb of Lazarus and says, "Come out" (Jn. 11:38-44). We are evangelists who trust in the sheer power of God's Word to raise the dead to life.

God-centered evangelism is a way of life. It does not advocate a method but encourages a knowledge of people and how to apply a macrogospel to the conscience. Witness should be natural, educational and bold. It is something we *are,* not just something we *do.* "Personal witnessing" is the phrase that best describes the evangelistic life to which all of us are called. Will you tell the truth?

Plans to Obey

By God's help, I plan in faith to respond to what I've learned about witnessing in the following ways (list *what* you are going to do, *how* you hope to do it and *when* you will begin):

Clearing My Conscience:
What has the quiet voice of God been saying to me? Is there a sin to confess? Is there a relationship that needs to be put right? Anything else?

Goals Regarding Non-Christians:
What is God calling me to do regarding non-Christians with whom I have a long-term relationship (such as family and friends)? What is God calling me to do regarding those with whom I have a short-term relationship (such as neighbors, classmates, business associates and people met in passing)?

Goals Regarding Christians:
What is God calling me to do with one other Christian to encourage and practice witnessing? How can I encourage my church or fellowship group to respond to God in evangelism?

Note: In appendix B, worksheets 11 and 12 give a sample program for an evangelism training seminar.

Appendix A
Complementary Approaches in Evangelism

Although this book deals primarily with individuals witnessing to other individuals, it is important to mention that there are other appropriate methods for a proclamation of the whole gospel.

Preaching

Obviously, this is one of the God-ordained means of evangelism (Rom. 10:14-15). Recent attempts in evangelicalism to focus on audience participation or drama (liturgy or activity) miss the mark. There must always be a focus on the message—the Word. There can and should be more flexibility and spontaneity in our services, but there should always be time for teaching and preaching.

When a man of God speaking out of a fresh experience of thankfulness and wonder brings a word from Scripture with power (the Spirit's unction), something takes place that communicates in a way few other things do. Many who have not been sent by God are giving stones instead of bread. To sit under Spirit-filled preaching is a convicting experience. Read some of the sermons of the Reformers and those in the Puritan tradition; you will be convinced.

There are many advantages in preaching; the speaker can go right to the heart and be very personal, yet minimize personal offense. A key is asking questions, getting the hearer to think, react and apply truth. A pastor need not always say "we" as he preaches, but should speak directly to his hearers bringing a word from God to the individual. The pastor can punctuate sermons with questions like these: "Why do you prefer sin? What is to be said for living the way you do? Why do you reject the Savior? Are you ready to meet God? Do you know the danger of putting off the matter?"[1]

Literature

We often meet people who will read but not talk. By loaning a book we reinforce what we have discussed in person. From my own experience I cannot think of an exception to the maxim: "Growing Christians are reading Christians." So with non-Christians. If they are willing to read, they are probably interested in the truth. There may be many reasons for carrying on a conversation with you or going to a Christian meeting—but studying in private indicates a real interest.

Choose your literature wisely. Some is appropriate for those who seem uninterested. Other types are good for active seekers. Think of the person's interests and needs and choose a book accordingly. Sometimes an autobiography is a good opener for it is readable and personal.

Giveaway literature should be provided by the body of Christians with whom you are associated. It should be visually attractive and well written. The impression made by such literature can either open or close the door for future witness. To have something to place in the hands of others gives you a good excuse for visiting their home or walking up to them in a park. It is a tool that can be used to initiate a conversation. I do not think much is gained by simply passing out hundreds of booklets as people rush by. Try to have a local name and address on the literature, or the time and place of a meeting. Most giveaway literature is not designed to contain the whole gospel but rather to raise a question or impress one crucial point in the receiver's mind. This topic can then form the basis for getting a reaction then or later. Just be sure you have read ahead of time what you give away.

We should have literature of deeper content available on a variety of contemporary issues and gospel points. An attractive book table, with some books at a discount (subsidized) displayed on campus or at a community fair, is a great evangelistic tool. Ironically, selling books can be more effective than giving them away: people are more apt to read a book they buy.

More Christians will use books in evangelism if they read more themselves. The most effective way to use literature is to say, "Here's a book that really helped me; I'd like to know what you think of it." Your excitement about a book will create more interest than a dozen advertisements. Therefore, every church and Christian group should have easy access to a bookrack or table. Some churches or groups are able to provide a library from which books can be borrowed.

The playing of messages on cassette tape in homes is another great opportunity to communicate. Even though you feel tongue-tied, you can bring in gifted people of God to help you preach the gospel and answer the questions of your non-Christian friends. Also a well-written letter to the editor of your local or campus newspaper will reach the attention of more non-Christians than advertisements (and it won't cost you anything!).

Small Groups
Sometimes people can be drawn out in an accepting, small group discussion. Being in a Bible study with others has been an avenue to faith for many. Although a teaching/leader-centered study can be helpful at times, non-Christians can relate much more easily to an inductive study. Here the Bible becomes the text while an initiator asks questions to bring out the facts, meaning and application of the passage. People are forced to read and think. They get involved with the Scriptures and begin to put themselves in the place of the writer or character discussed. A good leader will notice those who are learning and will challenge them by individually meeting with them. A good way to begin such a group is by personally inviting friends to a two- or four-week series in a neutral setting on a topic to which they can relate. Many evangelistic study guides are available from a local Christian bookstore.

Christian Hospitality

Although sharing our homes can permeate several other methods (and it is not just a method but an attitude), it should be singled out as a very important way to evangelize. We should open up our homes as well as our hearts to others. To invite people to be part of our lives and/or families is an important demonstration of the gospel in action. Dessert and a game of badminton might be more of a witness to some than a Bible study. We can share our interests with others, do things together, expose our marital needs and children's problems. Becoming involved with local government, the school, or community affairs and recreation programs may cause us to miss some weekday church meetings, but will give us the natural contact we need with non-Christians so that we can begin inviting them to our homes.

Large Groups

A variety of meetings and activities can directly expose people to the gospel. A well-presented lecture on abortion or euthanasia from a Christian perspective can stimulate someone to investigate what the Bible says. Films, plays and the development of multimedia shows by Christians are attracting non-Christian audiences. Street theater performances and recreational activities have put Christians into contact with those who would not otherwise come to anything religious. Christians with gifts can be creative and step out in faith. We should go where people are—they will probably not come to our places of meeting, especially if we have not already befriended them.

Corporate (Body) Witness

When Christians as a group get together, there is power. The Scriptures say that others shall know we are Christ's disciples by the love we display for each other. We should welcome unbelievers as observers in our fellowship communities where we speak not mere words but live concepts. Our brother-sister relationships are the dynamic equivalents for the truth we wish to convey. Repentance, faith, forgiveness, reconciliation, joy and struggle should all be evident within the Christian community. In the mouth of two or three witnesses God's Word is often confirmed. Nonbelievers can shrug off one Christian "kook," but when they continue to meet more, it starts them thinking! Indeed, it is questionable if evangelism can be done at all without reference to a Christian community.

Involvement in the World

Moved by compassion, we find that a corollary of our proclamation evangelism will be incarnation evangelism. That is, we will enter the world just as Jesus did when he helped people in spite of cultural and social barriers. For some of us this involvement could be on the individual level. We may find ourselves counseling someone with a marriage problem, adopting a child, taking care of elderly parents, or including an unwed mother or single parent in our family. We might help one friend find a job; another will need help in budget planning or have a need for some of our tools or books. Sometimes a teen-ager who cannot relate to his or her family will need a temporary place to stay. Other Christians might want to join in a cooperative action to attack various manifestations of evil and injustice that are at our doorstep, such as: honesty in politics, truth in advertising, love and discipline for abused children, protection for the unborn person, fairness in housing, personal care for the hospitalized and imprisoned. The list is endless.

Our witness as salt and light (Mt. 5:13-16) will lead to praise for our Father in heaven. It complements the gospel of the God who is the Creator and Redeemer, showing that he is concerned for the whole person. We become involved where people hurt because of the need and the rightness of our cause— not just to witness. We are thankful to do this as unto the Lord and rejoice when our finite compassion opens the door for an explanation of the infinite compassion of Jesus. Involvement in doing the truth is a part of telling the truth.

Appendix B
Worksheets for Improving Our Witness

Worksheet 1/Language Barriers

Explain the following terms in your own words, as if you were talking with someone who had no biblical background. Do not use any of the words listed in any of your explanations. Use synonyms where possible or a short phrase; no long sentences.

1. lost—

2. saved—

3. born again—

4. repent—

5. justified—

6. atonement—

7. propitiation—

8. spiritual—

9. holy—

10. sin—

11. salvation—

12. saving faith—

13. redemption—

14. believe—

15. God—

16. gospel—

17. the finished work of Christ on the cross—

18. invite Christ into your heart—

Worksheet 2/Personal Testimony

This is *your* spiritual autobiography. Many Christians are unable to point
to a crisis experience, or we do not always know the date when God brought
us into his kingdom (perhaps he did so when we were young). This does not
mean you have nothing to testify about. Be winsome, honest and
wholesome. Never go into detail about sins. After a person has heard your
story will they know basic truths about Christ, or only know you better?
Use *some* of the phrases under each heading to help you focus on important
things.

1. *What I Was Like:*
My family, friends, interest were. . . . My security (most important value)
was. . . . My religious background and attitude about Christ was. . . .

2. *What God Used to Begin to Open My Eyes:*
I was awakened to my need by (people, books, meeting, circumstances). . . .
What I thought and/or noticed (about myself, God, others) at this point was. . . .

3. *What It Was I Saw/Understood:*
Those aspects of the gospel that touched me were. . . . I came to understand
that Christ. . . . I saw my need was. . . .

4. *How Christ Has/Is Affecting My Life:*
My relationships with. . . . My attitude toward. . . . My desires now are. . . .
I'm now doing. . . . A difficult area of obedience is. . . .

Worksheet 3/Self-Image

One hindrance to witnessing is a distorted view of our own self-worth. This can take the form of either too high a view of ourselves (pride) or too low (despair). As you discover whether your self-esteem is high or low, take the findings from this worksheet to the Lord. It is his assessment that gives us the right balance.

1. I am a (one-word answers such as: student, female, carpenter, etc.)...

A.	E.	I.
B.	F.	J.
C.	G.	K.
D.	H.	L.

2. Some of my strengths (abilities, talents, gifts) are...

A.	E.	I.
B.	F.	J.
C.	G.	K.
D.	H.	L.

3. Some of my weaknesses (failures, recurring sins) are...

A.	B.	C.

4. I am motivated very often by (give one-word answers such as: duty, love, guilt, reward, truth; and then give an example of each)...

A.	B.	C.

5. I am afraid of...

A.	B.	C.

6. The main reason I do not witness more is...

7. Read Romans 5:1-5; 7:14—8:4, 15-17 and 2 Cor. 5:16-21 and write your personal reaction.

8. When God looks at me, he thinks of me as...

9. For additional help see: Anthony A. Hoekema, *The Christian Looks at Himself* (Grand Rapids, Mich.: Eerdmans, 1975), chaps. 1-5, 7, 10-12; John Bettler, "How a Christian Should View Himself" (Philadelphia: National Christian Publishers, 1978), two cassette tapes.

Worksheet 4/Listening and Questioning

Listening is hard work. It is active, not passive. Asking questions is an essential part of good listening. To ask good questions is to listen with your whole self involved. Listening is not something to try to fake; it must come from within. It is the way to give quality attention to others and the way to love them.

Evaluate one or two conversations you have had recently in the light of the following ideas about listening and questioning.

Poor Listener

☐ Assumes the subject is uninteresting.

☐ Focuses on the person's manner of expression (word choice).

☐ Becomes overstimulated; makes snap judgments.

☐ Listens only for the facts.

☐ Tries to outline the information.

☐ Fakes attention to the person.

☐ Is distracted by surroundings.

☐ Evades grappling with difficult information.

☐ Satisfied with only hearing what is first said.

☐ Lets emotional words or situations block information flow.

☐ Thinks about own response to what is being said.

Good Listener

☐ Finds something interesting in what is said and asks questions.

☐ Finds the message is always more important than grammar, sentence structure or wording.

☐ Listens rationally; evaluates but suspends judgment.

☐ Listens for the feelings too.

☐ Notes patterns, traits, principles and basic ideas.

☐ Shows disciplined attention through brief comments, reactions.

☐ Concentrates by focusing eyes and mind.

☐ Welcomes expression of difficult ideas or problems.

☐ Probes for the idea, assumption, problem behind the surface words.

☐ Maintains emotional control and is unshockable.

☐ Thinks about what is being said.

1. Evaluation of Conversation 1:

2. Evaluation of Conversation 2:

Worksheet 5/Prescription for Good Questions

Jesus was a master at asking questions (see how he helped Nicodemus in Jn. 3, the woman at the well in Jn. 4 and the man born blind in Jn. 9). Sometimes his questions are rhetorical; sometimes they are to expose the other person; sometimes they are to gain information; sometimes they are to give new insight.

Jesus also was constantly listening for the question behind the question. He does not directly answer questions but looks for what is behind them. This is how he handled questions like: Who's right when it comes to worshiping God (Jn. 4:20)? What do I have to do to be assured of living forever (Mk. 10:17)? Why was this man born blind (Jn. 9:2)? How can the new birth be true (Jn. 3:9)? We need this same skill in listening. We need to ask ourselves if we have really heard what people are saying when they ask questions or make strong statements.

One summer evening I was in a comfortable living room filled with amiable people engaged in after-dinner chit-chat. Because I am in a Christian ministry, sometimes people react very abruptly to anything I say. This particular night I was cornered and challenged by an intense older woman who kept returning to the same point in her conversation: "How could you believe in a God who would send people to hell?" I started to react with a reasoned statement on the nature of God. Then I caught myself and said, "You seem to react negatively. Has something happened to upset you?" Then I listened. Out came a story about a nonreligious close friend who had just died. Now I saw what was behind her hostile attitude. She didn't need a discourse on God's eternal hatred of sin; she was emotionally distraught. As I showed sympathy she became genuinely open to biblical counsel on several points. If we really wish to be friendly and helpful to people, whether we are thinking of group Bible study, personal counseling of Christians, witnessing, or raising our children, we need to learn the art of questioning. Here are some principles to keep in mind:

1. Take every possible chance to ask a searching question, then keep quiet. (When we're talking, we're not learning anything.)

2. One thoughtful question is worth a dozen inquisitive ones. The prod-and-pry approach makes people clam up.

3. Questions that come close to the other person's true interest get the best answers, provided we are interested.

4. Be prepared to wait. Sometimes a long silence can be more rewarding than another question.

5. In every case, the quality of an answer depends on the quality of attention given by the questioner.

6. Questions must spring from honest inquiry, not from attempts at flattery or efforts to manipulate the other person's thinking.

7. Questions that deal with a person's feelings are more provocative than those that deal with facts. Listen for and encourage all expressions of feeling.

8. What is our motive in asking questions? Are we just leading someone on in order to argue or to trap him or her, or do we really care for the person? Only a listening, loving heart can remove the mask we all wear.

Test Yourself

Some questions seem to close more doors than they open, while others lead to true dialog. Check the good questions on the following list, and mark the poor ones zero.

1. What did you do today?
2. Would you explain that to me?
3. How was the game?
4. How do you feel about that?
5. Is something the matter?
6. What would you have done?
7. Do you love me?
8. Why did you say that?
9. Oh, really?
10. For instance?

The odd-numbered questions are poor because they are conversation-stoppers, usually answerable in one or two words. The even-numbered questions are good because they call for thought-provoking answers that can send the conversational stone rolling and start others. They call for explanation and description and can lead to revealing a person's feelings and values.[1]

Worksheet 6/Friendship Evangelism

1. What are characteristics of friendship?

2. Think of one of your friends. What is it about him or her that you appreciate?

3. Think of two non-Christian (a, b) and two Christian (c, d) friends. Answer the questions (last 3 do not apply to Christians) in reference to these people.
How did you meet them?
a)
b)
c)
d)
What are two of their favorite interests?
a)
b)
c)
d)
How long have you known them?
a)
b)
c)
d)
Have you ever done anything of a non-religious nature with them? What?
a)
b)
c)
d)
Have they ever talked with you about a personal problem they are having?
a)
b)
c)
d)
How have you honestly shared yourself and one of your problems with them?
a)
b)
c)
d)

How often during each week do you spend time with them? What do you do when you are together?
a)
b)
c)
d)
How often do you pray for them? Are your Christian friends praying for them?
a)
b)
Have you ever spoken specifically to them about the Lord Jesus Christ?
a)
b)
Identify an obstacle each of them has to becoming a Christian. What could you say or do about this?
a)
b)
4. What will it cost to be a friend (Phil. 2:3-5, 20-21)? What barriers hinder you from giving yourself to others in friendship?

5. What is the relationship between friendship and witness (1 Thess. 2:7-12)? What approach to people displays how truly concerned we are to meet their needs (Lk. 24:17-19; Prov. 18:13, 15)?

6. What was Jesus' attitude toward people? To what extent was he concerned for his own personal interests and prestige (Mt. 9:36; 11:19; Mk. 10:45; Jn. 10:10-11)?

7. What have you learned about yourself as a friend through this exercise?

Worksheet 7/Discipling New Believers

We should attempt to meet one to one with people who have made a profession of faith regularly for a few weeks, keeping their focus on the scriptural basis for assurance and on Christ. We can do this by helping them learn how to begin reading Scripture regularly, praying with them in praise and confession, and giving them assignments. Assignments help to keep the focus off of us and our relationship with them (not that we're ashamed to be a model, but we want them to depend on God, not us).

In the first and second meetings go over the content of the gospel to clarify what has happened. It is important that this foundation be firmly laid before they go on to build the superstructure of the Christian life. New Christians need to see the importance of continuing each day to draw anew from the resources in Christ as justifier and sanctifier. We can focus on the person of Christ, the free grace of the Father's forgiveness and the full presence of the Holy Spirit to empower. We want to emphasize that the power needed for daily living is found by trusting in Christ in the present; it is not found by looking back to any past experience (even that of conversion) or seeking an additional experience with the Spirit in the future. We should give assignments to help new believers review the content and implications of the gospel and establish daily prayer and Bible reading. Take them with you to a small group Bible study and a Bible-teaching church.

In the third meeting, we can introduce them to materials that will systematically cover the basics of the Christian life (prayer, Bible study, fellowship, witnessing, fruit bearing, knowing God's will). We should discuss one topic each time we meet. We need to strike a balance in our meetings between spending time in covering the content of the basics and time in having them share problems and questions. And it's important to share our life and needs also. Agree to pray for one another.

Some books you could use are *Quiet Time, Right with God, I Want to Be a Christian, The Fight.*

Worksheet 8/Four Role Plays

A. Gospel Overview Presentation

Setting: Think of a non-Christian friend with whom you have had some opportunity to share certain aspects of Christian truth. This friend, by his or her
reactions (confusion, criticism, questions) obviously doesn't understand what
you're talking about.

Procedure: First person assumes role of a Christian and begins with a statement
similar to this: "You know, we've talked about Christianity a couple of times
but I get the impression that I'm not communicating what I really mean. Can
I give you an overview of where I'm coming from? Perhaps by giving you a frame
of reference for some of my statements we can communicate better.
How about hearing me out—saving your questions till the end?"

Second person assumes role of a semi-interested non-Christian. He or
she remains attentive for the presentation, not asking any questions, and
concludes by saying, "Interesting. Let me think about this and then we'll talk
some more." This person then gives feedback to the Christian on how well they
did/didn't do in expressing themselves.

Time: Overview of entire gospel—20 minutes. Bible can be used but not
notes. Evaluation of presentation—10 minutes. Evaluate content, illustrations,
body language.

Additional Ideas: You can switch roles and let the second person try if you add
an additional half-hour. You can take an entire hour with the second person
asking questions for clarification (not raising objections) instead of only remaining
silent during the overview.

B. Answering Questions of Non-Christians

Setting: There are about a dozen recurring questions which non-Christians ask
about the gospel. By beginning to get a handle on how to answer these,
you can both help people and steer the conversation back to the real question,
"What will you do with Christ?" While realizing that often these questions
are a smokescreen hiding their real self and needs, nevertheless there are times
when they are asked honestly. Pick one of the following questions:

1. Is the Bible trustworthy?
2. Is Christ the only way to God?
3. Why does a good God allow suffering and evil?
4. Isn't one person's opinion as good as another's in religion, since no
one can really know what is true?
5. I try to do my best, so won't my good efforts get me to heaven?

Procedure: First person assumes role of non-Christian asking one of the questions. Ask additional questions to clarify as needed. Second person tries to answer them.
Time: Dialog—15-minute minimum. Evaluation of answers—5 minutes.
Additional Ideas: Switch roles for the next 20 minutes. This exercise could also be done in small groups, that is with a number of others observing the dialog between two people.

C. Voicing the Objections of Your Non-Christian Friends

Setting: Think of a non-Christian friend or relative that you know well enough to know their objections to Christian beliefs.
Procedure: First person assumes role of their non-Christian friend, consistently reacting the way the friend would in the ensuing dialog with a Christian. First person begins by saying, "Well, my problem with Christianity is. . . ." Second person plays a Christian. The task is to listen and draw out the non-Christian and seek to answer.
Time: Dialog—15-minute minimum. Evaluation of each other—10 minutes.
Additional Ideas: Switch roles for the next 25 minutes. This is a good situation to include a third person who merely observes what the first two are saying and gives feedback to both.

D. Finding Out Someone's Level of Interest

Setting: Your non-Christian friend has been thinking about some of your talks together. He or she has actually started to become interested! But you don't know how much. How can you find out?
Procedure: First person plays role of one of their interested non-Christian friends. They pick *one* of three possible levels of interest without telling the other person what level is chosen: (1) intrigued enough to read a booklet; (2) interested enough to come to a Bible study; (3) wants to find out how to become a Christian. Maintain that level throughout the dialog. All questions and all statements should be made according to the appropriate level of interest. The goal of the second person is to find out how interested the other one is without immediately asking, for example, "Would you like to come to a Bible study?"
Time: Dialog—15 minutes.
Additional Ideas: Switch roles. Pray then and there for your non-Christian friends.

Worksheet 9/Questions Non-Christians Ask

In speaking of Christ to others, the same questions are raised again and again. These recurring questions are often a smokescreen to put us on the defensive or to throw us off the track. Usually the questioner is not asking with a sincere desire for an answer. To determine how important a question really is to the poser, ask, "If I answered that question to your satisfaction, would you consider becoming a Christian?" Many will quickly answer, "No, it's just something I'm curious about," or, "Not really, it's just a question I like to throw out to people." Depending on the background of the person, the amount of time you have and whether you perceive the question as crucial for the person, you can then adapt your answer. At times a short, biblical answer is best so you can get back to the really serious problems. For instance, when asked about the fate of the heathen, I will simply reply, "Will not the Judge of all the earth do right?" (Gen. 18:25). God is fair and everyone will be treated justly. It is unimaginable that there would be a scene in the afterlife in which a person shakes his fist at God, saying, "You didn't give me what I deserved!" The question is, "What have you done with the truth about God you have been privileged to hear?"

On the other hand, we should give honest and extended answers to honest questions, so we need to familiarize ourselves with the best in Christian apologetic literature. We must be willing to take time with people and bring them slowly along, if that is their need. Our confidence should never be in our ability to answer. It is better to say, "I don't know," than to try to give an uninformed answer. Even at best all our answers are partial. We cannot reason people into the kingdom, even though ours is a reasonable faith. Even to use evidences to establish the probability of Christianity achieves little. Since the mind of natural, fallen people is at enmity with God, the answer we give will not be palatable. For instance, have you ever heard someone object to the concept of hell? I have, and after the lengthiest and most cogent explanation that I could muster, I've had the questioner stare at me and say, "Why, I'll never believe in a God like that!" That response shows he is not really interested in truth or he would be willing to follow truth wherever it leads him, even though it cuts against his grain and he has to change his mind. Ultimately, the unresponsiveness of the questioner is not because of his intellectual misgivings, but rather is due to his moral condition. People do not come to the light because their deeds are evil (Jn. 3:19-21).

Here are twelve common questions asked by non-Christians. I have attempted to choose literature which will help us find answers. If we are able to express introductory answers to these questions, we will be a help to many people. Our own faith will be strengthened as we look more deeply into biblical teaching and develop fuller answers. It is important that we attempt to bring the answer to bear not only on the understanding of the questioner but also on his life and conscience as well.

1. Is the Bible Trustworthy?
F. F. Bruce. *The New Testament Documents: Are They Reliable?* Downers Grove: InterVarsity Press, 1960.

J. I. Packer. *Fundamentalism and the Word of God.* Grand Rapids, Mich.: Eerdmans, 1958.

2. Is Christ the Only Way to God?
J. N. D. Anderson. *Christianity and Comparative Religion.* Downers Grove: InterVarsity Press, 1970.

Brian Maiden. *One Way to God?* Downers Grove: InterVarsity Press, 1974.

3. What about the People Who Have Never Heard?
J. H. Bavinck. *An Introduction to the Science of Missions.* Philadelphia: Presbyterian and Reformed, 1960.

D. Steele and C. Thomas. *Romans: An Interpretive Outline.* Philadelphia: Presbyterian and Reformed, 1960.

4. Isn't One Person's Opinion as Good as Another's in Religion since No One Can Really Know What Is True?
Francis A. Schaeffer. *The God Who Is There.* Downers Grove: InterVarsity Press, 1968.

C. S. Lewis. *Mere Christianity.* New York: Macmillan, 1960.

5. I Try to Do My Best, So Won't My Good Efforts Get Me to Heaven?
Robert M. Horn. *Go Free! The Meaning of Justification.* Downers Grove: InterVarsity Press, 1976.

John Bunyan. *All of Grace.* Chicago: Moody, n.d.

6. Is Jesus God?
Leon Morris. *The Lord from Heaven.* Downers Grove: InterVarsity Press, 1974.

I. Howard Marshall. *The Origins of New Testament Christology.* Downers Grove: InterVarsity Press, 1976.

7. Doesn't Science Contradict the Bible?
Francis A. Schaeffer. *No Final Conflict.* Downers Grove: InterVarsity Press, 1975.

D. Martin Lloyd-Jones. *The Approach to Truth: Scientific and Religious.* Wheaton: Tyndale, 1964.

8. Why Does a Good God Allow Suffering and Evil?
R. C. Sproul. *The Psychology of Atheism*. Minneapolis: Bethany, 1974.
C. S. Lewis. *The Problem of Pain*. New York: Macmillan, 1943.

9. Life Is Meant to be Meaningless; Why Bother Trying to Find Answers?
James W. Sire. *The Universe Next Door*. Downers Grove: InterVarsity Press, 1976.
Francis A. Schaeffer. *Escape from Reason*. Downers Grove: InterVarsity Press, 1968.

10. Why Do I Need Religion?
Os Guinness. *The Dust of Death*. Downers Grove: InterVarsity Press, 1973.
Francis A. Schaeffer. *How Should We Then Live?* Old Tappan, N.J.: Revell, 1976.

11. Why Don't Christians Do Something about the Needs of People in This World?
Athol Gill. "Christian Social Responsibility" in C. René Padilla *The New Face of Evangelicalism*. Downers Grove: InterVarsity Press, 1976.
Francis A. Schaeffer. *Whatever Happened to the Human Race?* Old Tappan, N.J.: Revell, 1979.

12. Why Can't Christians Agree among Themselves?
D. Martin Lloyd-Jones. *The Basis of Christian Unity*. Grand Rapids, Mich.: Eerdmans, 1963.
R. C. Sproul. *Knowing Scripture*. Downers Grove: InterVarsity Press, 1977.

Worksheet 10/Guidelines for Organizing Contact Evangelism

1. Introducing the Idea.

As you invite people to join you in contact evangelism or as you train them, you will want to introduce a few basic concepts. Since we do not want to be only hearers of the Word, it is necessary to place ourselves in insecure situations in which we must lean hard on God. We are not saying that contact evangelism is the only way or that everyone will be equally gifted at it. But it is right to seek for opportunities with strangers and it is an important training experience for Christians in developing an ongoing life of evangelism. Jesus said, "I will make you fishers of men." Let's throw out our nets broadly, expecting God to give a response. We do not need to manipulate or force people; we merely tie in with the work that God is already doing in the hearts of those we meet. He always goes before us. We never go alone. We need to learn how to be friendly, how to draw people out, how to confront them with the truth in a loving way.

2. Moving Out.

Work out and announce details of where you are going, how to get there, when to return for prayer and sharing. Explain that you will work in pairs and look for individuals or couples to approach (unless you are contacting people who have visited your church or fellowship group). Some possibilities are: house visitation, beaches, parks, literature tables, or during lunch times at work or school. If it is a business or school, be sure you have asked the advice of any Christians who may already be ministering there, plus cleared your plans with the proper authorities. Distribute giveaway literature. Mention the importance of getting names and/or recording reactions for future follow-up. Pray and pair up.

3. The Encounter.

A. A good opening question is essential. Here are a few possibilities:

1. "Here's some literature we're giving away. It's free. By the way, what's your religious background?"

2. "We're asking people for a few minutes of time so we can find out their opinions on some important matters. Could you spare a few minutes to answer some questions?"

3. "We're interested in finding out what people know about some of the main teachings of the Bible. Could you answer a few questions?"

4. "We're approaching people today to find out what they think about spiritual or religious matters. Most people are either hostile, indifferent, or open to spiritual things. Could you tell us which you are? Why?"

B. A good idea for continuing the conversation, after the initial exchange of your questions and their answers, is one of the following:

    1. "What you've said interests me. I've found that many people today have bits and pieces of religious knowledge but no clear and concise understanding of the theme of the Bible. Many people have found it helpful to hear a brief summary of this theme. I'm prepared to take fifteen minutes to go over it with you right now. Could we do that? I really think you'd find it helpful." Then present an outline of the gospel.

    2. "What you've just said interests me. I'd like to know more about why you think that way. I wonder if you've ever considered this as an answer (or alternate view) to the point you just made. . . ." After picking up on a point they have made and really listening to them further, ask them if they would in turn give you fifteen minutes to try to give them a frame of reference for what you have been saying. Give them an overview of the gospel using your outline.

C.   Ask them to consider these things seriously. Leave appropriate literature. Ask if you can come back again to bring them an answer to (or literature about) a question they raised. Set up a definite time. Get their names and phone number so you can call the day you are to meet them to make sure they are in.

4. Evaluation.

A.   What did you learn from this experience?

B.   How will you apply what you learned?

Worksheet 11/Schedule for a Weekend God-Centered Evangelism Training Seminar*

Friday Night

7:30   *Session 1*—Personal testimony(ies) on attempts at witnessing. Personal witnessing defined (pp. 19-27).

8:30   *Session 2*—The gospel reduced (chapter 2).

9:15   Prayer partners or prayer groups—hand out materials, overview of schedule.

9:30   Conclude

Saturday

8:15   Quiet Time—Acts 17:22-34; Philippians 3:4-9. Compare Romans 7:7-14. (See worksheet 15, studies 1 and 2.)

8:45   *Session 3*—The gospel recovered: part one: outline, points 1, 2, 3, (pp. 43-62). Discussion.

9:45   Break

10:00   *Session 4*—Jesus breaks the barriers to witness. (Small group Bible study. See worksheet 14, study 5.)

11:15   Break

11:30   *Session 5*—The gospel recovered: part two: outline, points 4 and 5 (pp. 62-74). Discussion. Prayer groups or prayer partners.

12:30   Lunch

2:45   *Session 6*—Introduction to witnessing (pp. 119-33). Feedback from any lunchtime witnessing experiences.

4:00   Individual study time: Memorize *The Greatest Test: Overview* and review your written testimony.

4:30   *Session 7*—Meet in pairs to role-play a gospel presentation and your testimony. Evaluate each other. (See worksheets 2 and 8A.)

5:30   Dinner

7:00   *Session 8*—Questions non-Christians ask: communication principles (worksheets 8B, 8C, 8D, 9). A panel format works well for this session. (Use material on pp. 118-33.)

8:30   Prayer partners or prayer groups.

9:00   Conclude

Sunday

8:15   Quiet Time

8:45   *Session 9*—The normal Christian evangelist (pp. 110-17). (Small group Bible study. Worksheet 15, study 4.)

(Page references and worksheets are from Tell the Truth.)

9:45	Break
10:00	*Session 10*—Christian boldness and the conscience of others (pp. 133-41). Discussion.
11:30	Plan to obey (p. 154, in pairs). These can be shared briefly with whole group. Conclude with prayer and singing.
12:30	Lunch

Preseminar Assignment: 1. Write out your personal testimony (four minutes), using worksheet 2 or gospel outline. 2. Memorize the gospel outline in *The Greatest Test: Overview.* 3. Pray that God would lead you to someone to witness to.

The weekend format is designed for use as a weekend retreat. The format may be adjusted to be held at a church location. In this case the Sunday sessions would be altered to coincide with the Sunday-school hour (session 9) and the worship service (session 10 in a sermon form). Schedules for three Saturdays or twelve sessions over twelve weeks follow.

No evangelism training is complete without field experience. Sometimes this can be built into the weekend itself if it is sponsored by a campus ministry such as InterVarsity Christian Fellowship. Meals can be taken in student dining halls and contact evangelism done in pairs. Otherwise, participants should sign up for visitation evangelism in the neighborhood or back on campus. Accountability is important.

Tell the Truth *by Will Metzger, InterVarsity Press. A training manual in the message and methods of God-centered evangelism. Available through your local Christian bookstore or at the address below.*

The Greatest Test *by Will Metzger. A booklet for training Christians in the content of a God-centered gospel. Available from: Great Christian Books, 1319 Newport Gap Pike, Wilmington, DE 19804 (302-990-0595).*

Worksheet 12/Memorizing the Content of the Gospel

This page contains an overview of *The Greatest Test* gospel outline in a handy format for memorizing and review. Every Christian should know the gospel inside out, thoroughly and accurately. You will then be free to listen to what others are saying and bring in various aspects of the gospel more naturally. This outline is not to be used mechanically, but creatively. Some people may want to familiarize themselves with the Bible passages that tell a story under each point so they can "storytell" the gospel.

We call people to respond to a person, Jesus, yet a contentless Jesus could be molded to our wishes. The New Testament represents conversion as not only a response to a person, but to truth. [Obey the truth (Rom 6:17); believe the truth (2 Thess 2:12-13); acknowledge the truth (1 Tim 2:4, Jn 8:32).] Peaching the gospel is called proclaiming the truth in 2 Cor 4:2.

THE GREATEST TEST: OVERVIEW

1 God the Test-maker 1. Maker-owner 2. Father 3. Judge.
Point: God has rights over man; man accountable.
Bible: Paul's sermon—Acts 17:22-34; Mt 5:48; 1 Pet 1:15-16.
Illustration: The inventor.
2 God's Test 1. Two rules 2. God knows best 3. Be like him.
Point: God's perfect standard measures all actions/attitudes.
Bible: Rich man—Mk 10:17-27; Mk 12:30-31, Jas 2:8-13.
Illustration: A high-jumper has limits.
3 Mankind Fails the Test 1. Disobedience is sin 2. Sin is like a disease 3. Sin must be punished.
Point: Not met the requirements, so separated from God.
Bible: Peter realizes sin, Lk 5:1-11; Rom 3:20, 23; Rom 8:7-8; Is 59:2.
Illustration: The Gap between God and sinners.
Question: Can you admit you're a sinner?
Dilemma: How to get right with God?
4 Jesus Christ the Substitute Teacher 1. God becomes man 2. Jesus scores 100 for us 3. Jesus is sin-bearer for us 4. Jesus rises and offers himself to us.
Point: Jesus is sinner's Substitute-Reconciler, Lord, Savior.
Bible: Crucifixion and resurrection—Jn 19:17—20:31; Rom 8:3-4; Mk 10:45; 1 Pet 3:18.
Illustration: Jesus bridges gap; and a pencil erases failing grade, marks perfect score.
5 Your Response: 1. Personal response commanded 2. Turn from sin 3. Trust in Christ.
Point: Receive Christ as your Savior and Lord.
Bible: Foolish, wasteful son—Lk 15:11-24; Acts 17:27, 30; Rom 10:9-10; Ps 51:17.
Illustration: Pencil offered must be accepted to be received.
Only three possible responses—Acts 17:32–34.

The Greatest Test *is available in booklet form from: Great Christian Books, 1319 Newport Gap Pike, Wilmington, DE 19804 (302-999-0595).*

Worksheet 13/Suggested Schedule for Three All-Day Evangelism Training Seminars

First Seminar Day

8:00   Quiet Time—Acts 17:22-34; Philippians 3:4-9. Compare Romans 7:7-14.

9:00   *Session 1*—Personal testimony(ies) on attempts at witnessing. Personal witnessing defined (pp. 19-27). Prayer groups or prayer partners.

10:15   Break

10:30   *Session 2*—The gospel reduced (pp. 28-41). Include examples of problems in modern evangelism. Discussion.

12:30   Lunch

1:30   *Session 3*—The gospel recovered: outline, God and man (pp. 43-62). Discussion.

3:00   Break

3:30   Individual Study Time: Prepare your own gospel outline or memorize the sample.

4:30   *Session 4*—Meet in pairs to role play a gospel presentation and evaluate each other. (See worksheet 8A.)

6:00   Dinner

7:30   *Session 5*—The gospel recovered: Christ and response (pp. 62-74). Prayer groups or prayer partners.

Assignment: Read text, parts one and two and appendix A. In appendix B complete worksheets 1, 2, 3. Review gospel outline and attempt to explain it to someone.

Second Seminar Day

8:00   Quiet Time—Mark 4:1-20; 2 Corinthians 4:1-18; 5:11—6:10.

9:00   *Session 1*—Conversion of the total person (pp. 75-84). Talk on small group Bible study.

10:15   Break

10:45   *Session 2*—The whole gospel to the mind, emotions and will (pp. 85-104). Discussion.

12:30   Lunch

1:30   *Session 3*—Personal testimony(ies) on attempts at witnessing. Brief review of part one (pp. 22, 32-33, 41, 72-74). Introduction to methods of witnessing (pp. 105-10).

2:45   Break

3:15   *Session 4*—The normal Christian evangelist (pp. 110-17). Small group Bible study.
4:15   Individual Study Time: Review gospel outline and/or do worksheets 2, 3 and 4.
6:00   Dinner
7:30   *Session 5*—How to communicate personally (pp. 119-33). Discussion.

Assignment: Review text, parts one and two. Complete worksheets 4, 5, 6. Read part three. Review gospel outline and attempt to explain it to someone.

Third Seminar Day
8:00   Quiet Time—1 Thessalonians 1:1—2:13.
9:00   *Session 1*—Personal testimony(ies) on attempts at witnessing. Prayer for those witnessed to. Review briefly parts one and two. How to communicate personally (pp. 133-49).
10:15 Break
10:45 *Session 2*—Panel or role play on questions non-Christians ask. (See worksheets 8B and 9.) Brief talk on speaking to the conscience (pp. 137-41).
12:30 Lunch
1:30   *Session 3*—Guidelines on contact evangelism. (See worksheet 10.) Pray together.
2:00   Contact evangelism experience.
5:00   *Session 4*—Sharing of the afternoon's experiences in evangelism.
6:00   Dinner
7:15   *Session 5*—Small group Bible study on John 4:4-42.
8:15   Fill out "Plans to Obey" (p. 154), individual reflection time.
8:45   *Session 6*—Short exhortation on our goal: disciples and worshipers (pp. 149-54). Conclude with singing, sharing and prayer.

Assignment: Implement your "Plans to Obey." Read worksheet 7 and complete final two role plays (C and D) on worksheet 8. Do any worksheets uncompleted. Read *Evangelism and the Sovereignty of God*, J. I. Packer and *Out of the Saltshaker*, Becky Manley Pippert.

Worksheet 14/Suggested Schedule for a Twelve-Session Evangelism Training Seminar

Session 1—Intro. to the seminar (pp. 11-18). The normal Christian evangelist (pp. 107-17). *Assignment:* Self-image worksheet (p. 161) and read chapter one.

Session 2—Personal witnessing defined (pp. 19-27). *Assignment:* Personal testimony worksheet (p. 160) and read chapter two.

Session 3—The gospel reduced (pp. 28-41). *Assignment:* language barriers worksheet (p. 159) and read chapter three.

Session 4—The gospel recovered (pp. 42-72). *Assignment:* Memorize gospel outline and do role play A (p. 168). Read Romans 1—5.

Session 5—Sin defined (pp. 49-61). *Assignment:* Review gospel outline and ask a non-Christian to hear your gospel outline. Reread chapter three. Read chapters four and five.

Session 6—Conversion of the total person: mind (pp. 75-86). *Assignment:* Worksheets on pp. 165-66. Read chapters six and seven.

Session 7—Conversion of the total person: emotions and will (pp. 90-102). *Assignment:* Two worksheets on pp. 162-63. Read pp. 118-30.

Session 8—Practical ideas in witnessing (pp. 118-30). *Assignment:* Role plays C & D (p. 169). Read pp. 130-49.

Session 9—Practical ideas in witnessing (pp. 130-49). *Assignment:* Write a letter explaining the gospel to a non-Christian friend. Read pp. 149-54.

Session 10-Doing evangelism: Take class time to share witnessing experiences and pray for people by name. Discuss p. 173. *Assignment:* Read appendix A and skim worksheet 9 (pp. 170-72).

Session 11-Doing evangelism: Do role play B (p. 168). Choose one or two objections to discuss as a group. *Assignment:* Review gospel outline. Explain to a Christian or non-Christian. Read p. 167.

Session 12-Prayer and the Spirit: Review pp. 113-17 from session 1. Share experiences, pray. Fill out p. 154. *Assignment:* Ask someone in the group to pray and hold you accountable for your "Plans to Obey," calling you every two weeks for three months.

Allow one hour minimum for each session. The materials should not be presented on consecutive days unless the participants have time to do the assignments. While a Sunday-school setting is possible, allowing 1½ to 2 hours per session will give more time for discussion and prayer. Assignments given at each session are for the *following* session. Participants should do evangelism in pairs, possibly through neighborhood visitation. See guidelines (p. 173).

Worksheet 15/Supplemental Bible Studies and Review Questions

Study 1: What Is God Like? *(Use with chapter three.)*
Introduction: Paul's sermon in Acts 17:22-34 is in response to his contact with people in a setting similar to our relativistic religious world. Many used the term *god* but filled it with their own meaning. Paul starts with what he observes about them and then moves quickly to distinguish the true God from their false gods. He proclaims (not argues) because God reveals himself. In the Old Testament, God progressively revealed his nature and character. His names were one means by which he did this. The names "I Am" and "Jehovah" speak of him as self-existing, self-determining and sovereign to the Hebrew mind. Is Paul now communicating the same truth about God in different terms to the pagan mind? *Read Acts 17:22-34.*

Vv. 22-23—Were these people atheists? What kind of ideas might they have had about God? Why can Paul be dogmatic about God?

Vv. 24-28—Paul begins to define the word *God* positively. What is God like? List and elaborate on everything these verses tell you about God.

V. 29—Paul concludes this view of God with a negative definition. What is God not like?

Vv. 30-31—What is now added to our understanding about God?

Vv. 25-31—In describing God, Paul has occasion to comment on man. What can you find in these passages about man? What is implied about the relationship of man with God?

Vv. 32-34—What three reactions do people have to this view of God in Paul's preaching? Can you think of similar examples of these today?

Study 2: What Is Sin? *(Use with chapter three.)*
Introduction: Communicating the idea of sin is essential to right witnessing. For many people sin is a blurred concept. This results in a lack of conviction when that word is used. Just as with the word *God,* we have to restore biblical content to the word *sin.* Sin, to the modern mind, is either looked on too lightly ("Everybody makes mistakes." "I couldn't help it." "It was only a white lie.") or only as referring to monstrous acts (massacres, torture and the like). Therefore, the modern conscience is eased by these faulty definitions since either "everybody does it" or "other people have done much worse things than I." When a weak definition of sin is combined with a sentimental view of God (lover of all and punisher of none), no wonder most unbelievers see little need of forgiveness (Christ as Savior) or release from the mastery of sin (Christ as Lord). For those who do not see their guilt, the story of Paul (who trusted in adherence to an external standard and did see the pervasive nature of his sin) is illuminating.

Read Philippians 3:4-9.

V. 4—What does "confidence in the flesh" mean?

Vv. 5-6—What does Paul cite as the basis of his security and acceptance before God? Give contemporary examples in each of his categories.

Vv. 7-8—Why had Paul previously considered all these things as profit (gain)? Why does he now say he thinks of them as unprofitable (loss)?

Vv. 8-9—Why is Christ now so important to Paul? What is righteousness based on law? What is righteousness based on Christ? What has Christ to do with Paul's righteousness?

This was a huge turnaround for Paul. Let's turn to the next passage to see what brought him to it.

Read Romans 7:7-14.

V. 7—How did Paul discover he was *not* blameless (faultless, sinless)?

Vv. 8-14—Which commandment in particular gave him trouble? What part of our "actions" are exposed by the tenth commandment? What do you covet?

What is the purpose or function of the law? Does the law create sin? What does Paul mean when he says the commandment produced death?

Can anyone then use the law as a ten-rung ladder to climb up to God? Why not?

What do most people today equate sin with? What is sin according to the Bible?

Compare and read aloud as a summary: Rom. 3:19-28 and 4:4-7, 22-25.

Study 3: Parable of the Four Soils *(Use with chapter four.)*
Read Mark 4:1-20.

Vv. 1-8—To get the facts firmly in mind, review the four soils and what happened to the seed sown in each.

Vv. 9-12—Why did Jesus teach in parables? The fact that some people have "ears to hear" and others do not reminds us of what facts about God? About people? About God's revelation in the Bible?

Vv. 13-20—Ask someone to define each of the images in the parable as Jesus does (The seed is . . . , etc.).

What happens in the first soil? Give contemporary examples.

What happens in the second soil? Give contemporary examples.

What happens in the third soil? Give contemporary examples.

What is characteristic of the fourth soil? What is signified by fruit or crop? [Note: Many people assume this refers to converts produced by our witnessing. However, the normal meaning for "fruit" in the New Testament is that of the "fruit of the Spirit" (Gal. 6:22-23).]

How should the fact that there are different soils (conditions of the heart) in unbelievers influence our methods of evangelism? What implications are there for the content of our evangelistic message?

Can you think of other examples in Scripture where there seemed to be a response to the gospel, but it wasn't lasting?

Study 4: Called to Serve in Weakness *(Use with chapter five.)*

Introduction: We have examples in both the Old and New Testaments of God's ministry being carried out by very ordinary people. Their weakness becomes a strength. When they are humbled, they can more faithfully rely on God and more clearly see him as the enabler. A strong sense of the call of God, the rightness of what we are doing, and love for others stabilize them for a consistent Christian witness.

Read about Moses (Ex. 3:1-14; 4:10-17).

3:10—What does God want Moses to do?

3:5-9—What aspects of God's character and purpose are stressed? What might the burning bush in verse 2 symbolize?

3:11-12—What is Moses' *first* objection? Can you mention a similar fear you have? What is God's answer?

3:13-14—What is Moses' *second* objection? Whose response is he concerned about? What is God's answer? (In 4:1-9 we also see a *third* objection and God's answer.)

4:10-12—What is Moses' *fourth* objection? In what ways do you try to escape responsibility? What is God's answer?

4:13-17—What is Moses' *fifth* objection? What is God's answer?

Read about Timothy (2 Tim. 1:5-8; 2:1-2).

1:5—Describe Timothy's Christian background.

1:6-8—What is implied about Timothy in these verses? What is shame? Why are we afraid of the opinions of others?

1:6, 8; 2:1-2—What does Paul want him to do? Would this have been easy for him?

Read Jeremiah 1:4-9 and 2 Corinthians 12:9-10 as a conclusion.

Study 5: Jesus Breaks the Barriers to Witness *(Use with chapter nine.)*

Introduction: In John 4 Jesus witnesses to a stranger (social barrier) who is a woman (sex barrier) who is also a Samaritan (religious barrier)! He is never condescending, but rather asks help of her. Moving from a common concern on the physical level (water, thirst), he develops a conversation about spiritual matters. He never compromises the truth, but moves into the conscience showing this woman her need. (The Samaritans were an unorthodox sect of Jews.)

Read John 4:4-42.

Vv. 4-9—What kinds of barriers does Jesus cross? What need does Jesus have? What do you make of the woman's reaction?

Do you find it hard to be friendly to others? Why? Do you admit your needs to others? Why not? What barriers (sex, culture, religion, age, education and so on) do you find it hard to cross? Why?

Vv. 10-15—How did Jesus turn the conversation to spiritual matters? Can you give examples from everyday life of how you have (or could) do the same?

On what two levels is this conversation proceeding? Why did the woman want the water?

Vv. 16-24—Describe what Jesus is doing in verse 16. How do you account for the question she brings up? Explain Jesus' answer.

Vv. 25-42—What attitude is implied in the woman's response? How do you think she felt after Jesus' statement?

Afterward how did she describe Jesus (vv. 29, 39)? Why is this significant?

How did others become believers (vv. 28-30, 39-42)? What sustained Jesus (vv. 31-38)?

Study 6: Our Manner and Methods as Whole Evangelists
(Use with chapter eight.)
Introduction: Paul exemplified the kind of whole person we should be as we seek to bring the whole gospel to bear upon the entire life of a nonbeliever. He spoke the truth in a loving way. He was persistent and patient. These passages give us a glimpse into the man and his methods. Glean from them ideas to apply to yourself.
Read 2 Corinthians 4:1-18; 5:11—6:10.

4:1-6—How might we be tempted to use deception in witnessing? How might we be tempted to distort the Word of God? How can we speak to the conscience? Why don't we lose heart? What two things does the passage say about "ourselves"?

4:7-18—What phrases in Paul's description of a minister-evangelist strike you? In what ways do you see death "at work" in you? What reason is now given for not losing heart?

5:11-15—What two motives for witness do you find here?

5:16-21—How is the ambassador metaphor appropriate for witnessing?

6:1-10—What two expressions does Paul use in describing himself and his friends as minister-evangelists? How is the urgency of salvation expressed?

What did it cost Paul to be a fellow worker and servant of God? What has it cost you?
Read 1 Thessalonians 1:1—2:13.

1:1-10—Why is Paul so thankful? How does Paul know that God has chosen (elected) these people (that they have saving faith)? What results of regeneration are mentioned?

2:1-6—What are some temptations to have an improper ministry? Paul calls on God to be his witness in examining his ministry. Could we do the same? Is our conscience clear?

2:7-9—What did Paul do beyond speaking the gospel to them? What does he compare his ministry to?

2:10-13—How might these people have witnessed Paul's holiness, righteousness and blamelessness? What imagery does Paul use here?

Paul concludes the way he has begun—with thankfulness. What two instruments did God use in drawing the Thessalonians to belief?

Close by reading 2 Corinthians 2:14-17.

Study 7: Review Questions

Part One.

1. Explain each phrase in the theme: The whole gospel to the whole person by whole people.

2. Which do you consider more important to understand, the content of the gospel or the methods of communicating the gospel? Why?

3. What are some elements of the gospel that need to be recovered?

4. Critique this statement: We just preach Christ; we don't get into theology in evangelism.

5. What part does a presentation of the law of God and sin have in evangelism?

6. How do feeling sorry for your sins and repenting of them differ?

Part Two.

1. Give an example from Scripture of a "partial" conversion.

2. What three aspects of the personality are affected in regeneration? Why is this important?

3. What is saving faith?

Part Three.

1. Define evangelism.

2. List the four pivotal points of the gospel and at least two Scripture references to support each.

3. What kind of attitude and motivation should characterize a Christian when evangelizing?

4. What is the place of prayer in evangelism?

5. What are some questions or comments you can use to turn a conversation toward Christianity?

6. What has been most helpful to you in this book?

Notes

Introduction

[1]Carl F. H. Henry, "The Purpose of God" in *The New Face of Evangelicalism*, ed. C. René Padilla (Downers Grove: InterVarsity Press, 1976), p. 31.

[2]Kenneth S. Latourette, *A History of the Expansion of Christianity*, vol. 1 (New York: Harper and Brothers, 1944), pp. 116, 169, 230, 233ff.

Chapter 1

[1]Kenneth Prior, *The Gospel in a Pagan Society*, (Downers Grove: InterVarsity Press, 1975), p. 51.

[2]There are three primary words in the New Testament for proclaiming the Christian message: *euaggelizesthai* (tell good news); *kerussein* (proclaim); and *marturein* (bear witness). The English words *evangelism* and *gospel* come from the same Greek word: *euaggelion*. This word is composed of two words meaning "good" and "news." Therefore, to evangelize is to set forth the good news. The context usually shows that it includes a demonstration or doing as well as a proclamation or saying. For a thorough study of the three words see chapter three in Michael Green's *Evangelism in the Early Church* (Grand Rapids, Mich.: Eerdmans, 1970).

[3]J. I. Packer, *Evangelism and the Sovereignty of God* (Downers Grove: InterVarsity Press, 1961), p. 56; see also pp. 37-45.

[4]D. Martyn Lloyd-Jones, *The Presentation of the Gospel* (London: Inter-Varsity Fellowship, 1949), pp. 6-7.

Chapter 2

[1]"Truly the essence of the apostolic method was not some all-consuming effort to reach as many different people as possible with the message, but rather, subject both to the leading and enablement of the Holy Spirit, the first-century Christians labored in a strategic center until a nucleus of believers was formed into a local church. Evangelization was not some truncated message of the plan of salvation, but a declaration of the whole counsel of God. It was then left to the local company of Christians to maintain continuing evangelism in their community." C. Stacey Woods, "God's Initiative and Ours," *I.F.E.S. Journal* (1966), 4.

[2]Packer, pp. 47-49.

[3]Some roots are found in the techniques developed by the revivalist Charles Finney.

[4]This is not to say that we shouldn't rejoice whenever Christ is preached (even if the motives are wrong), as Paul did (Phil. 1:15-18). But when there is a distortion of Christ and his salvation, we must object as Paul also did (Gal. 1:6-9).

[5]"Meet My Friend" (Westchester, Ill.: Good News Publishers, n.d.), n. pag.

[6]A. W. Tozer, *The Old Cross and the New* (Harrisburg, Pa.: Christian Publications, n.d.), n. pag.

[7]George Sweeting, "What Is Your Favorite Game?" (Chicago: Moody Press, n.d.), n. pag.

[8]Tozer, n. pag.

[9]David T. Smith, "You're a Beautiful Person" (Chicago: Moody Press, n.d.), n. pag.

Chapter 3

[1]Green, p. 70; see also p. 250.

[2]Another form for organizing the content of the gospel can be derived from summarizing the history of redemption. This historical or covenantal framework would begin with God as the Creator and covenant maker, and present the key events sequentially, concluding with Christ's exaltation.

[3]See Green, chaps. 2—5 and Prior.

[4]C. S. Lewis uses the powerful imagery of Aslan the lion to convey a biblical view of God. "But as for Aslan himself, the beavers and the children didn't know what to do or say when they saw him. People who have not been in Narnia sometimes think that a thing cannot be good and terrible at the same time." C. S. Lewis, *The Lion, The Witch, and The Wardrobe* (New York: Collier, 1970), pp. 116-17.

[5]Packer, pp. 60-61.

[6]Ibid., pp. 62-63.

[7]"The law is not to be rejected because a man has no power to keep it. When the rejection of the law is argued on this ground, it is often forgotten, that similarly, man has no power to obey the gospel. The command to believe is as impossible as the command to obey, and so the Gospel seems to speak just as impossible things as does the law. Absence of ability does not infer absence of obligation. . . . But it is an unreasonable thing to conceive of the law apart from the Spirit of God, and then to compare it with the Gospel; for if the Gospel itself—even its promises of mercy and forgiveness—were to be thought of apart from the Spirit, it would achieve nothing: indeed, by itself it would be as much a dead letter as the law. But neither the law nor Gospel is a dead letter, for the Holy Spirit makes use of both in a saving manner." Ernest Kevan, *Moral Law* (Grand Rapids, Mich.: Sovereign Grace Publishers, 1971), pp. 10-11.

[8]Rebecca Manley Pippert, *Out of the Saltshaker* (Downers Grove: InterVarsity Press, 1979), chaps. 4—6.

[9]John Bunyan, *Pilgrim's Progress* (Grand Rapids, Mich.: Zondervan, 1967), pp. 33-34.

[10]For an excellent and readable discussion of the relation of the Christian to the Law, see Horatius Bonar, *God's Way of Holiness* (Chicago: Moody), n.d.;

Walt Chantry, *God's Righteous Kingdom* (Edinburgh: Banner of Truth, 1980).

[11]I owe these three points to Rev. Al Martin of Trinity Baptist Church in an unpublished sermon on repentance.

[12]Francis A. Schaeffer, *Death in the City* (Downers Grove: InterVarsity Press, 1969), pp. 70-71.

[13]"True believers may have the assurance of their salvation divers ways shaken, diminished, and intermitted; as by negligence in preserving of it; by falling into some special sin which woundeth the conscience and grieveth the Spirit; by some sudden or vehement temptation; by God's withdrawing the light of His countenance, and suffering even such as fear Him to walk in darkness and have no light. . . ." *Westminster Confession,* Chap. 28, Sec. 4.

[14]A third type of person would be someone who lacks assurance simply because they do not believe in the doctrine of assurance. That is, they do not think Scripture teaches even the possibility of a person knowing with certainty they are redeemed and will be taken to heaven. They dismiss such ideas as conjecture and pride.

[15]G. I. Williamson, *The Westminster Confession of Faith; A Study Guide* (Philadelphia: Presbyterian and Reformed, 1964), p. 133.

[16]Ronald Wallace, *Calvin's Doctrine of the Christian Life* (Grand Rapids, Mich.: Eerdmans, 1962).

[17]A continuation of repentance and faith constitutes the life of the Christian. The fruits of repentance are the extension into our lives of the essence of repentance. Spurgeon commented that repentance to be sincere must be perpetual, for it is not an act but the acquisition of an attitude. Calvin refers the origin of repentance to faith, but does not posit a time lapse during which it brings it to birth. He means to show that a man cannot apply himself seriously to repentance without knowing himself to belong to God. *Institutes* III, 3:3, 5.

[18]Packer, p. 71.

[19]Robert Horn, *Go Free,* (Downers Grove: InterVarsity Press, 1976), pp. 117-19. Compare Horatius Bonar, *God's Way of Peace* (Moody, n.d.); John Owen, *Justification by Faith* (Grand Rapids, Mich.: Sovereign Grace, 1971).

[20]Francis A. Schaeffer, *The God Who Is There* (Downers Grove: InterVarsity Press, 1969), p. 169.

[21]It is interesting to note that within Pentecostal and Third-World circles some of these same themes are being sounded. Juan Carlos Ortiz of Argentina contends for an evangelism that is not man centered, calls for obedience to Christ as Lord, and refuses to call people Christians who show none of the biblical distinctives. *Disciple* (Carol Stream, Ill.: Creation House, 1975).

[22]Walt Chantry, *Today's Gospel—Authentic or Synthetic?* (London: Banner of Truth, 1970), p. 17.

Chapter 4

[1]The term *conversion* is often defined as the individual's initial response of faith and repentance. Sometimes the Puritans used terms to describe the order of various aspects of the Spirit's work. A sinner went from *awakening* (a new sensitivity to God) to *seeking* (looking for answers) to *conviction* (felt guilt) to *conversion* (faith and repentance).

[2]Green, pp. 159-61, 204-06.

[3]Joseph Hart, "Come, Ye Sinners, Poor and Wretched," 1759.

[4]These are adapted from Peter Masters, *Physician of Souls* (London: Wakeman, 1976), pp. 110-25.

Chapter 5

[1]Even true Christians entering the secular campus have a rough time, especially if their religious background has emphasized only feelings and fellowship. Nevertheless, if God calls them to this situation, spectacular growth often follows.

[2]All doubt is not sinful. See Os Guinness, *In Two Minds* (Downers Grove: InterVarsity Press, 1976).

[3]Bernard Ramm, *The Witness of the Spirit* (Grand Rapids, Mich.: Eerdmans, 1960), p. 89.

[4]John Stott, *Balanced Christianity* (Downers Grove: InterVarsity Press, 1975), p. 13. See also John Stott's excellent book *Your Mind Matters* (Downers Grove: InterVarsity Press, 1973).

[5]Calvin taught the priority of knowledge in faith, but did not advocate spiritual intellectualism. He felt that the will could not act nor the emotions respond until they both had been enlightened by the intellect. Abraham Kuyper, *The Work of the Holy Spirit* (Grand Rapids, Mich.: Eerdmans, 1975), p. 263.

Chapter 6

[1]Stott, *Balanced Christianity*, pp. 17-18. However, even in some of the most theologically orthodox groups there is a paucity of praise. Some of the Scripture turned into songs by the Jesus people and Pentecostals can help us learn how to weave emotion together with music, focusing on grace.

[2]For example, Philip Swihart's *How to Live with Your Feelings* (Downers Grove: InterVarsity Press, 1976) and the writings of Walter and Ingrid Trobisch, James Dobson and David Augsburger.

Chapter 7

[1]Andre Bustanoby, "An Open Letter to Jane Ordinary," *Christianity Today*, 16 Mar. 1967, p. 14.

[2]"It is the citadel of the will which has to be stormed, and if he is wise, the evangelist will approach this fortress neither by the avenue of the mind alone, nor by the avenue of the heart alone, but by both." John

Stott, *Fundamentalism and Evangelism* (Grand Rapids, Mich.: Eerdmans, 1959), p. 58.

[3]Lloyd-Jones, p. 9. I owe many of the thoughts in this paragraph to this out-of-print, British IVF booklet.

[4]Joseph Hart, "Come, Ye Sinners, Poor and Wretched," 1759.

[5]For a helpful discussion see Packer's *Evangelism and the Sovereignty of God.*

[6]J. I. Packer in the introduction to John Owen, *The Death of Death* (London: Banner of Truth, 1959), pp. 1-25.

[7]Compare D. Martyn Lloyd-Jones, "Mind, Heart, and Will" in *Spiritual Depression* (Grand Rapids, Mich.: Eerdmans, 1965).

[8]John Bunyan, *Pilgrim's Progress* (Grand Rapids, Mich.: Zondervan, 1967), p. 82. See also the conversations with Hopeful and Ignorance.

[9]Often the New Testament represents conversion in terms of our response not to a person but to the truth. It is to obey the truth (Rom. 2:8; 6:17; 1 Pet. 1:22), to believe the truth (2 Thess. 2:12-13) and to acknowledge or come to know the truth (Jn. 8:32; 1 Tim. 2:4; 4:3; 2 Tim. 2:25; Tit. 1:1; 1 Jn. 2:21). Similarly, to preach the gospel is not just to proclaim Christ but to manifest the truth (2 Cor. 4:2). See John Stott, *Your Mind Matters,* pp. 49-50.

Chapter 8

[1]Lloyd-Jones, *The Presentation of the Gospel,* p. 3.

[2]For an evaluation of the results of contemporary mass evangelism, see *Eternity,* September 1977, including C. Peter Wagner, "Who Found It?" pp. 13-19; James F. Engel, "Great Commission or Great Commotion?" p. 14; Lynn Holman, "Here's Living Proof," p. 19.

[3]For a readable discussion on being yourself and emulating Jesus in evangelism, see Rebecca Manley Pippert, *Out of the Saltshaker* (Downers Grove: InterVarsity Press, 1979).

[4]Dr. C. John Miller, *Basic Guidelines for Witnessing* (Westminster Seminary, Class Syllabus), pp. 11, 13.

[5]*Reformed Evangelism* (Grand Rapids, Mich.: Baker, 1962), pp. 140-42.

[6]Roger Barrett, "Motives for Witnessing—Good or Evil," *Christianity Today,* 17 July 1970, pp. 12-14.

[7]Miller, p. 7.

[8]"We find it difficult to witness because we have not learned to be open. Being real means being free to express ourselves when it is *appropriate* to do so." John White, *The Fight* (Downers Grove: InterVarsity Press, 1976), pp. 67-68.

[9]Packer, pp. 122-25.

Chapter 9

[1]For example, E1 = Evangelism among your own people (Jerusalem and Judea). E2 = Evangelism among people different from you, yet still of your language and country (Samaria). E3 = Evangelism among people who are different in language and race (uttermost parts of the earth). Donald McGavern and Win Arn, *How to Grow a Church* (Glendale, Calif.: Regal, 1973), pp. 51-53.

[2]Charles Bridges, *The Christian Ministry* (London: Banner of Truth, 1959).

[3]Definitions by Brooks Alexander, "What Is a Cult?" *Spiritual Counterfeits Project Newsletter,* January/February 1979, pp. 2-3.

[4]Paul Little, "How to Win Souls to Christ," *Presbyterian Journal,* 13 Jan. 1965, p. 10.

[5]Horn, pp. 120-21. Some questions leave a wrong impression: "Why not try Jesus?"; "Can you think of any reason to not become a Christian?"

[6]Little, p. 37.

[7]James Kennedy, *Evangelism Explosion* (Wheaton: Tyndale, 1970), p. 21.

[8]I owe the material in this section to Donald C. Smith, "Conversational Evangelism," unpublished paper. It can also be found in Pippert, pp. 143-45.

[9]All thought is based on assumptions which cannot be "proved." So as Christians, we begin with God who reveals truth to us.

[10]Francis A. Schaeffer, *The God Who Is There* (Downers Grove: InterVarsity Press, 1969) and Os Guinness, *The Dust of Death* (Downers Grove: InterVarsity Press, 1973) are both good for an overview. The many writings of Dr. and Mrs. Schaeffer taken together will beautifully illustrate the balance between taking the mind seriously and humbling it. They also portray the connection between truth and living out the truth.

[11]The law of God written in the heart as described in Romans 2 is probably different from conscience. Nevertheless, the law seems to use the faculty of conscience to express itself. Some people are so degenerate that their conscience is cauterized (1 Tim. 4.2), or defiled (Tit. 1.15).

[12]Will Barker, from an unpublished sermon.

[13]John Bunyan, *Pilgrim's Progress* (Grand Rapids, Mich.: Zondervan, 1967), p. 130.

[14]C. H. Dodd cited in Green, pp. 60-64.

[15]"A Christian who perseveres with a stereotyped approach *may* meet with some success. Sooner or later he will presumably encounter someone to whom the way in which he presents the gospel applies. Furthermore, knowing what we do about the sovereign grace of God, we may expect

him to see that a dedicated evangelism will be rewarded by a contact that fits his approach." Prior, p. 41.

[16]J. I. Packer, "What Is Evangelism?" *Theological Perspectives on Church Growth,* Harvie Conn, ed. (Presbyterian and Reformed, 1976), p. 91.

[17]*Lausanne Covenant,* Clause 4.

[18]Ramm, p. 71.

[19]Green, p. 85.

[20]Helmut Thielecke, as quoted by Green, p. 79.

[21]Lloyd-Jones, *The Presentation of the Gospel,* p. 15.

Appendix A

[1]Masters, see his excellent chapter, "A Plea for Gospel Sermons." Cf. Al Martin, "What's Wrong with Preaching Today?" (London: Banner of Truth, 1975).

Appendix B

[1]"Ask, Don't Tell," *Christian Herald,* August 1966.

Cultural Globalization

For *John MacDonald Wise,*

Intrepid traveler,
bemused parent